Authority
and
Democracy

By the same author :

Political Theory of Anarchism
Direct Action and Liberal Democracy

29199

Authority and Democracy

April Carter
Somerville College, Oxford

Routledge & Kegan Paul
London, Henley and Boston

First published in 1979
by Routledge & Kegan Paul Ltd
39 Store Street,
London WC1E 7DD,
Broadway House,
Newtown Road,
Henley-on-Thames,
Oxon RG9 1EN and
9 Park Street,
Boston, Mass. 02108, USA
Set in Times Roman by
Computacomp (UK) Ltd, Fort William, Scotland
and printed in Great Britain by
Redwood Burn Ltd
Trowbridge and Esher

British Library Cataloguing in Publication Data

Carter, April
    Authority and democracy
    1 Authority
    I Title
    301.5'92   JC571   78–40862

ISBN 0 7100 0090 1

Contents

Introduction

Authority is a concept central to social and political thought, and yet its precise nature remains remarkably elusive. There are a number of reasons for this elusiveness. One is the ambiguity and complexity of the uses of the word in ordinary speech, indicated, for example, by the very different connotations attached to the two adjectives associated with authority: authoritative and authoritarian. A second source of ambiguity is the fact that we apply the concept of authority to a number of very different spheres of social activity: to the sphere of knowledge as well as the sphere of politics; to relations in the family and school as well as the factory or army; and both in novels and everyday life we recognize the authority of a strong personality. Whether we regard all these forms of authority as different manifestations of one quintessential type of social relationship which we call authority, or whether we believe that political authority is different in kind from authority in, for example, education depends in part on our broader understanding of politics and society.

One of the most fundamental disagreements between theorists of authority is whether authority, like religious faith and tradition, was part of a world we have now almost wholly lost, leaving the contemporary world with a crisis of authority; or whether authority has changed its accoutrements but still exists in modern form in modern industrialized and rationalist society. Sociologists and political theorists who espouse the first view turn their gaze to the aristocratic order of Europe prior to the French Revolution, when social life was governed primarily by deference to hierarchy, by custom and by unreflecting prejudice. Robert Nisbet elaborates on the picture of this society delineated by nineteenth-century social theorists in his book *The Sociological Tradition*. The most celebrated exponent of the second point of view is Max Weber, who accepted the importance of tradition as a source of authority but looked for an alternative type of authority, and alternative grounds for it, in the modern bureaucratic state in an increasingly rationalist world.

1

Interpretations of authority necessarily vary with the political philosophy of the writer. A preliminary distinction can be made between conservative theorists, who have always tended to uphold existing forms of authority and to maintain the necessity of authority for social stability and the preservation of a civilized mode of life; and liberal, socialist and anarchist theorists, who view authority with varying degrees of distrust. Liberal rationalists see authority usurping the individual right to autonomous thought and decision, socialists see authority as an ideological gloss on the injustice of class rule, and anarchists usually see all forms of authority as a source of social corruption. Radicals in general have associated authority with authoritarian control which minimizes personal freedom: the fact that our predominant image of authority comes from the hierarchy of a traditional and aristocratic type of society reinforces the reactionary connotations of the idea of authority.

There are good reasons to suspect the exercise of authority in the contemporary world. If authority is defined, as it often is, as a relationship in which those in authority can evoke automatic and unthinking obedience, then there have been numerous occasions when the plea of obedience to orders has been used to justify the most terrible crimes. A recent well-known psychological experiment, described by Stanley Milgram in a book entitled *Obedience to Authority*, demonstrated how an alarming number of participants in the experiment obeyed orders to give electric shocks to individuals, even when they believed that these shocks were causing great pain and could be lethal. There are also good reasons to suspect the calls for the reassertion of authority which are evoked by fears of widespread political revolt, of increasing crime statistics and of the breakdown of accepted morality among the young. Calls for more authority, whether in the home, the school, the university, the factory or the state, usually disguise the desire to enforce obedience and to impose stern discipline in order to stop permissiveness and anarchy undermining the social order.

There is, however, a serious conservative case for authority which is far removed from a crude recourse to authoritarianism, and which emphasizes the role of authority in upholding not only moral and intellectual standards but also in guaranteeing social and political freedom, and acting as a barrier to centralized, arbitrary and despotic power. This case is argued in three recent contributions to political theory – Hannah Arendt's essay on Authority in her book *Between Past and Future*, Carl Friedrich's study of *Tradition and Authority* and Robert Nisbet's reflections on *The Twilight of Authority* – although each elaborates a slightly different conception of authority. All three writers are in some sense conservative, though this label obscures as much as it illuminates. If all are hostile to radical egalitarianism and to the Marxist tradition, each has sympathy with aspects of progressivism: Arendt's belief that true politics is exemplified in direct democracy and heroic action makes her responsive to certain styles of revolutionary politics; Friedrich has a liberal faith in reason; and Nisbet is sympathetic to the pluralist version of anarchism propounded by Proudhon and Kropotkin. All pose a challenge to radicals prepared to dismiss the question of authority as irrelevant.

It is arguable that radicals should not be less interested in the nature and role of authority than conservatives, but more so. The problem of authority is a problem for radicals precisely because they are committed to change; they need to ask whether and in what spheres it is possible to dispense with authority altogether and to consider the peculiar difficulties of trying to create new forms of authority. Furthermore the very nature of authority, if it is defined as the ability to evoke purely voluntary compliance, suggests its importance to anyone interested in how to preserve social peace without recourse to violence.

This book is conceived both as a dialogue with Arendt, Friedrich and Nisbet about the nature and implications of authority and as a series of provisional reflections on the possible forms of authority, its importance for various spheres of social and political activity, and the problems of maintaining or re-creating authority after social change or political revolution.

Chapter 1
Authority in the Ancien Régime

One way of trying to understand authority is to look for models of authentic authority in a historical and social context. This approach has two advantages: it is illuminating about the social customs, attitudes and beliefs which have been historically associated with the phenomenon of authority; and it makes explicit the hazy images of the past which influence our commonsense understanding of authority. Several possible images of authority can be derived from previous societies, but the most central image that we inherit is of hierarchical authority in the aristocratic order of Europe before the French Revolution, in which authority was inherent in the relationships between superior and subordinate within an ordered gradation of rank. The concept of aristocratic society, coined by De Tocqueville to denote the social order of the ancien régime, is more precise than the broader and more abstract concept of community usually favoured by sociologists.

The Ideal Type of Aristocratic Society

The ideal type of aristocratic society is characterized by strict hierarchy of social status, age and sex. The social hierarchy is maintained by a willing acceptance of this order of society, a unifying set of values and a world view which enshrines and legitimizes hierarchy. Its morality is largely unreflecting, expressed through customary modes of action, through etiquette and through generally accepted prejudices.

Within aristocratic society one of the most central forms of authority is that of the patriarchal head of the household. De Tocqueville, when exploring the distinctions between the old aristocratic society of Europe and the democratic society of the new world of America, noted that one characteristic difference lay in the nature of the family. In America, he remarked, 'the family in the Roman and aristocratic signification of the word does not exist', and he went on to define the typical form of the

4

family in Europe (*Democracy in America*, p. 230):

> In aristocracies, then, the Father is not only the civil head of the
> family, but the organ of its traditions, the expounder of its customs,
> the arbiter of its manners. He is listened to with deference, is
> addressed with respect and the love which is felt for him is always
> tempered with fear.

In this type of aristocratic family not only is the father set apart, but the
children are all graded by their age and sex into different ranks with
distinct privileges and obligations.

One of the most vivid descriptions of the head of an aristocratic family
is given by Giuseppe di Lampedusa, who portrays the traditional values
of the House of Salina in Sicily at a time when the old order is under
assault from Garibaldi's rebel army and the more insidious influences of
the modern age. The novel starts with the Prince conducting prayers for
the household, but a more telling ritual is that of the dinner-table (*The
Leopard*, p. 20):

> Dinner at the Villa Salina was served with the slightly shabby
> grandeur then customary in the Kingdom of the Two Sicilies. The
> number of those taking part (fourteen in all, with the master and
> mistress of the house, children, governesses and tutors) was itself
> enough to give the dining-table an imposing air ... When he entered
> the dining-room, the whole party was already assembled, only the
> Princess was sitting, the rest standing behind their chairs. Opposite
> his own chair flanked by a pile of plates, swelled the silver flanks of
> the enormous soup tureen with its cover surmounted by a prancing
> Leopard. The Prince ladled out the minestra himself, a pleasant chore,
> a symbol of his proud duties as paterfamilias.

The hierarchy of the household was a microcosm of the order of
society, a society in which pupils were subordinate to their teachers,
apprentices to their masters, commoners to the nobility, laymen to the
clergy, subjects to their sovereign, and everyone to their God. The social
belief in the inevitability of hierarchy can be extended beyond the human
sphere to embrace the heavenly and natural world as well. Medieval
Christian philosophy elaborated a cosmology which specified the
gradations of degree in God's universe, stretching down through the
several orders of angels and other heavenly beings to man and to the
lower forms of animal and plant life. It is this world view which Burke
evokes, in a more general and abstract form, in passages of the
Reflections, in particular the famous passage which opens 'Society is
indeed a contract ...' and culminates in an appeal to 'the great primaeval
contract of eternal society ... connecting the visible and invisible world'
(*Reflections on the Revolution in France*, pp. 194–5).

There are two important points to note about the nature of authority
within the ideal type of aristocratic society. The first is that the idea of

authority, far from being sharply defined, is so diffuse that it is possible to dispense with it altogether in delineating the various social relationships. Consider Burke's rhetorical enumeration of the blessings of English society compared with the anarchy and despotism experienced in France:

> We fear God; we look up with awe to kings; with affection to parliament; with duty to magistrates; with reverence to priests; and with respect to nobility (p. 182).

The attitudes of veneration and deference and a sense of duty can be adduced to explain why people obey their superiors without recourse to the concept of authority as such. Robert Nisbet, in his characterization of authority in aristocratic society, suggests that 'authority is hardly recognized as having separate or even distinguishable identity'. He comments (*The Sociological Tradition*, pp. 107–8):

> Deeply embodied in social functions, an inalienable part of the inner order of the family, neighbourhood, parish, and guild, ritualized at every turn, authority is so closely woven into the fabric of tradition and morality as to be scarcely more noticeable than the air men breathe.

The second point about authority relationships in aristocratic society is that they are necessarily based on social and economic coercion and often entail the use of considerable force. In the patriarchal family, where the father enjoyed his unquestioned right to command, the wife was economically and legally subject to her husband, and the children were often punished harshly for disobedience; in the wider society pupils and apprentices were strictly disciplined by their masters, priests threatened their flocks with dire supernatural retribution for disobedience, and the resources of the law and the force of the state could be invoked to keep the lower orders in their place.

Whether aristocratic society is delineated primarily in terms of unreflecting obedience based on habit, deference and duty or in terms of social, economic and political repression depends largely on the political views of the interpreter. Conservatives naturally stress the element of voluntary respect and radicals the element of coercion. An image of authority derived from aristocratic society must clearly allow for both the subordinate's sense of duty to obey and the superior's ability to enforce obedience. This concept of authority also entails belief in the right of those in superior positions to give orders to those below them, a right which is inherent in the very fact of the social hierarchy, although it may be justified in addition by appeal to tradition, religion or the order of the universe. The adjective corresponding to this form of authority is 'authoritarian'.

There is, however, quite a different model of authority which can be discovered in aristocratic society: that is the authority of wisdom, learning or skill. The authority of the old over the young can be justified by their experience and greater knowledge, while the authority of the teacher or master craftsman is explicitly based on specialized knowledge and skill. This kind of authority is intrinsically different from hierarchical authority: it does not depend on social status but on the respect accorded a tradition of knowledge and the expertise of the individual practitioner, and it confers not a right to command in the strict sense of the word but the right to convey information or to give counsel. The adjective corresponding to this form of authority is 'authoritative'.

Within aristocratic society the distinction between hierarchical authority and the authority based on special skill or knowledge was blurred because the social order tended to assimilate the two kinds of authority in a single role. The teacher and the master craftsman were placed in authority over their pupils. Parents' right to guide their children because of their greater age and experience could not be disentangled from their natural superiority in the social hierarchy. Moreover there is a sense in which the organization of aristocratic society tended to create special ability, and therefore a right to make authoritative decisions. So long as social arrangements ensure that men are better educated and more experienced in most spheres of life than women, and that the nobility do, in some sense, represent the best in society, then the authority accruing to men and the well-born tends to seem right and natural.

Pluralism and Freedom

A picture of aristocratic society which highlights the hierarchical and authoritarian nature of social relationships suggests at first glance a society which allows very little freedom. Yet aristocratic society is represented by a number of political theorists as a society guaranteeing political and social freedom, and both Robert Nisbet and Hannah Arendt suggest there is an intrinsic connexion between the kind of authority embodied in hierarchical society and the preservation of freedom. This connexion becomes clearer when it is observed that the ideal type of aristocratic society can yield a very different conception of authority – a conception which distinguishes between authority limited to a specific sphere and the claims of a potentially all-embracing sovereign power. This focus on social pluralism lays less stress on the relationships within institutions like the family than on the relations between various autonomous institutions – family, guild, university and church – and the state. The pluralist view of aristocratic society is contrasted with alternative types of unfree society – Hannah Arendt compares it with the equality of all subjects before their ruler and the total lack of liberty entailed in the Greek model of tyranny, and Nisbet compares it with modern democratic despotism.

Nisbet suggests that after the French Revolution conservative theorists saw two types of society to be in conflict with each other: the aristocratic type in which the power of the central government was limited by the independence of the aristocracy, by the autonomy of social, economic, educational and religious bodies and by the decentralization of power to local political bodies with customary and legal privileges; and the emerging society in which the destruction of custom and privilege in all its forms and the abolition of social rank left all citizens equally helpless before the inroads of despotic power exercised by a centralizing government. The first type of society can be encapsulated in the idea of 'social authority' – and what this means above all is a society in which there is a plurality of bodies with their own spheres of interest, values and jurisdictions and their own authorities – as opposed to the spectre of all-encompassing political power presented by the state which lays claim to jurisdiction in all spheres and tolerates no competing or independent authorities: the state as envisaged in Hobbes's *Leviathan*.

Theorists who draw on the model of aristocratic society necessarily associate pluralism with the existence of social hierarchy and in particular with an aristocracy. In this context the aristocracy can be seen as playing several different roles. De Tocqueville stresses the aristocracy's social role in upholding and promoting a set of cultural standards and their political role in acting as a check on central monarchial power, and hence as a guarantor of political pluralism, in an idealized aristocratic society; though they had failed to fulfil this political function in France prior to the Revolution. Because he was not primarily concerned with the social status of the aristocracy, De Tocqueville could explore the possibility of a pluralist and free society in an egalitarian and democratic context in America, and despite his misgivings about the spread of equality he did not claim social hierarchy was always and intrinsically necessary to political freedom. Burke on the other hand defended the aristocracy not only as a bulwark against despotic government but also because he attributed to them superior political skill and saw social deference to rank as a necessary element in political stability. It is Burke's eloquent defence of English society against the terrors which sprang from social levelling in France that suggests an inextricable link between social hierarchy and the enjoyment of constitutional liberties. It is a Burkean view of the world that Nisbet consciously evokes in his book *The Twilight of Authority* and he quotes Burke to deplore the disrepute into which the word hierarchy has fallen and urges that the philosophy of pluralism is rooted 'in frank recognition of the value inherent in hierarchy' (p. 238).

Burke can be cited as an exponent of the connexion between authority and freedom because of the nature of English society and government which he was concerned to defend. The social hierarchy in late eighteenth-century England was not wholly rigid, so that the individual was not necessarily bound to the station in life defined by his birth, and

Burke does not argue simply for an aristocracy of the blood but for an aristocracy of dignity and talent that implies a degree of openness at the top. Moreover Burke was upholding a constitutional and partially representative form of government in which the crown was circumscribed within agreed limits and in which the individual could claim inherited rights and liberties. Burke is the most persuasive of conservative political theorists not only because of the eloquence of his writing but because of the moderation of his general position and the liberal elements in his conservatism.

The Problem of Restoring Aristocratic Authority

It is instructive to compare Burke with the French political theorists of conservatism writing after the Revolution, Bonald and De Maistre. They are more truly theorists of a pure ideal type of aristocratic society, in which the political authority of the sovereign is an extension of the patriarchal authority of a father over his family and the monarchy crowns the social hierarchy. The French conservatives bring out clearly the coercive nature of authority relationships in a strictly hierarchical society and they also illustrate the peculiar problems facing theorists who seek to 'restore authority' in a society where many of the social and political bases for hierarchical forms of authority have been destroyed.

Bonald and De Maistre hoped to restore order by reasserting the sanctity of rank, the monarch's absolute right to rule and the overarching religious domination of the Catholic church. Bonald's conception of the family stressed the unconditional obedience due to the husband by his wife and to their parents by the children; his ideal society was based on the relationship between a hereditary nobility and a loyal peasantry – industrialism was to be shunned as one of the factors disturbing traditional patterns of life and belief and undermining social stability. Bonald argued for absolute monarchy, attacking the very conception of a division of powers as one of the causes of division in the body politic and a prelude to revolution. The social and political bounds of this restored aristocratic society were to be cemented by the religious unity imposed by the Catholic church: Bonald regarded diversity of religion as a source of civil discord, so both freedom of religion and freedom of thought should be suppressed in favour of true religion. Catholicism had the added merit of promoting unconditional political obedience, whereas in Bonald's eyes the doctrines of protestantism encouraged free-thinking individualism and so were inherently subversive of social order and loyalty to superiors.

Bonald therefore was a theorist of absolutism and an opponent of individual freedom. But absolutism did not imply that total or arbitrary power could be wielded by the sovereign, who was constrained by obedience to the will of God, by awareness of the importance of respecting the natural ordering of society and by a sense of duty towards his people. Monarchical absolutism was bound by tradition to respect the autonomy of spheres of social authority – of the family, guild and church. Authority in Bonald's theory implied an absolute right to command obedience, but within a clearly defined sphere,

De Maistre also desired a restoration of the ancien régime under an absolute monarch acknowledging the spiritual authority of the pope, though he was prepared to concede that the appropriateness of a form of government depended on the social conditions in a country. De Maistre is distinguished from other conservative theorists by his much greater readiness to emphasize the necessity of physical and spiritual violence and by the cynicism with which he prescribes the benefits of religion. In a celebrated passage of the 'St. Petersburg Dialogues' he invokes the executioner and torturer as a pillar of the social order (p. 192). and he suggests too that the most important reason for a religious restoration is that it will help to keep the masses obedient through fear of supernatural tortures to come. De Maistre's God appears to be primarily a God of violence. who promotes war in order to exact divine vengeance for human iniquity (pp. 251–4). Despite his detestation of the rationalism of the philosophes, De Maistre's political reflections draw heavily on Rousseau and in particular on Rousseau's concept of sovereignty. De Maistre accepts that there may be a division of governmental powers, as in England, but formal sovereignty is achieved when these powers are in agreement and there are then no limits to their power. It is logically inevitable that sovereignty should be absolute and should be unlimited (pp. 112–13). In his treatment of sovereignty De Maistre is closer to Hobbes and Rousseau than to the conservative theorists of limited authority and social pluralism.

A comparison of Burke, Bonald and De Maistre suggests two major conclusions. The first is that authority is not compatible with absolutism. If authority can only exist when its sphere is delimited and if authority is associated with a degree of political freedom, then political authority can only be found in constitutional régimes, where there are explicit and enforceable limits to governmental power. De Maistre's concern is not with political authority but with sovereignty maintained by force, and although there is an element of pluralism in Bonald's picture of society it is extremely questionable how far political absolutism can allow real freedom or how the political sphere can be confined in practice – indeed De Tocqueville analysed in some detail how the ancien régime in France prior to the Revolution had undermined social pluralism and had strengthened centralized political power. The second conclusion that can be drawn is that it is unrealistic to try to re-create a hierarchical form of authority when social change has undermined the bases for this kind of social order, and that attempts to do so necessarily involve resort to violence and suppression of freedom. Bonald's proposals for restoring not only the monarchy but an aristocratic form of society were wholly impractical after the political and social rupture with the past brought about by the Revolution and in the light of general economic and social trends, as subsequent French history shows. De Maistre was more realistic but also more radical in his emphasis on the role of violence in creating order in a context where stability could no longer be ensured by continuity of tradition and of the social values upholding aristocratic society. De Maistre illustrates one of the points underlined by Hannah Arendt in her essay on Authority: that when authentic authority is lacking, the exponents of authority and order will often try to put violence in its place.

The Loss of Authority?

Political theorists who associate stable authority with aristocratic society tend to the view that authority has been irretrievably lost in the modern world. If authority is identified with acceptance of social hierarchy, then it is by definition incompatible with a fully democratic and egalitarian society. Although our society has not achieved equality, belief in natural hierarchy does look increasingly irrelevant. This sense of irrelevance is illustrated by the rejection of what once appeared to be immutable biological reasons for hierarchical relationships between men and women, parents and children. Once social hierarchy in general has ceased to seem natural, the facts of sex or age do not automatically create a right to command obedience.

The authority that is based on knowledge is not intrinsically incompatible with democratic and egalitarian attitudes and beliefs, and it can be argued that while the authoritarian models of the father of the patriarchal family or the aristocrat have become outdated, the equally archetypal models of the wise man, the teacher and the professional craftsman are still relevant. But social change can destroy this kind of authoritativeness. The authority of wisdom based on experience is eroded if the past ceases to be a reliable source of knowledge in the present, and if social values alter, so that the old and young lose confidence in the relevance of the former code of beliefs and behaviour. If change is sufficiently rapid then not only do the old lose their former claim to wisdom, but adults lose their confidence to teach children about the world. Change can also make traditions of learning or skill appear outmoded or inappropriate.

Social trends in Western Europe have tended to undermine social hierarchy and traditions simultaneously. It is therefore understandable both that we should tend to identify secure authority with the ideal type of aristocratic society and that we should assume that the authoritarian and authoritative forms of authority are necessarily interrelated.

One possible objection to trying to maintain a practical as opposed to a purely analytical distinction between non-authoritarian and authoritarian types of authority is that the former is dependent upon a hierarchical order, because respect for authority cannot survive unless there is a general predisposition to deference and respect for superiors. To take a popular example, it is often argued that loss of respect for adult authority in general means that children will cease to respect the professional authority of their teachers. This argument appears to have some basis in historical evidence. It is for example suggestive that the trend towards the disappearance of all forms of social authority has gone further in the United States than in Europe, where aristocratic culture and social hierarchy held sway longer and still exert some influence. But it is questionable whether there is a necessary connexion between respect for special knowledge or wisdom and the existence of an authoritarian hierarchy. It could be argued that the real basis of authority in a hierarchical society is not the hierarchy itself, but the customs and beliefs which uphold that social order and unite society. Thus respect for authority stems primarily from a stable set of values, which we have historically associated with aristocratic society. It is also possible to claim that this historical model has tended to destroy understanding of true authority by confusing it with coercive power and claims to absolute and unthinking obedience, and that the belief that all authority is authoritarian has promoted hatred and distrust of any kind of authority.

Chapter 2
Defining Authority

Two central concepts of authority can be derived from aristocratic society: authority based on special knowledge and authority based on special status in a social hierarchy. The nature of authority which stems from wisdom or professional expertise has not changed in contemporary society. Hierarchical authority, in the original sense, only exists in very attenuated forms, but it has – as Weber asserted – been replaced by a bureaucratic authority in which people hold commanding positions in various organizational hierarchies. Bureaucratic authority entails a relationship between a superior and subordinates and a right of command, and it can be reinforced by various forms of coercion, so it is similar in significant respects to aristocratic authority. In both cases it is appropriate to speak of being in a position of authority.

Being in authority is often understood to mean the right to command obedience, including the right to enforce obedience when necessary. T. D. Weldon suggested that 'force exercised or capable of being exercised with the general approval of those concerned is what is normally meant by "authority" ' (*The Vocabulary of Politics,* p. 54). Most theorists who have recently tried to define authority have however agreed that the nature of authority is best understood if it is distinguished from the other methods of influencing behaviour, and that it should therefore be distinguished from force or violence. This approach not only contrasts pure authority with pure forms of violence, for example the violence of a highwayman who demands your money or your life, but with the kinds of legal force used by governments.

Whether authority implies the right to use force or is an alternative to force is the first question to be decided in defining authority. If authority rests on voluntary consent, then logically it appears to be an alternative to force which relies on fear to secure obedience, or else literally enforces it. If authority is contrasted with force, then it raises the most interesting questions for social theory, since it follows that a social group or political

13

body in which there is widespread respect for authority should be able to maintain itself with minimum resort to force, if not dispense with it altogether. This book therefore defines authority in contradistinction to force, though problems about the link between the two in practice must be discussed later. So what we normally understand as being in authority implies two different kinds of relationship: a pure authority which can evoke willing compliance, and a power to command and enforce obedience. For the rest of this chapter the term 'being in authority' is used to denote only the relationship of pure authority.

Authority must also be distinguished from the form of influence which is at the opposite pole from violence – persuasion. Persuasion may rely on reason or on emotion, but whatever the motives and methods involved persuasion means convincing someone solely through the strength of the arguments used. To recognize authority is to be persuaded in advance that whatever is advocated will be worthy of respect and of compliance.

Third, authority must by definition be differentiated from the type of influence which appeals to self-interest through promises, incentives and bribes. If authority is fully accepted then obedience is a response to authority – there is no need for further inducement. Bribery is moreover, in its nature, incompatible with authority. Recognition of authority implies respect for the person or office with authority, whereas one does not respect the offerer of bribes, if bribery implies encouragement to do wrong. Authority may be more compatible with offering fair incentives or rewards for good behaviour, but it is still a quite different form of influence.

Finally, any preliminary definition of authority must make clear that recognition of authority entails a belief in the right of the authority figure to issue commands or judgments. The notion of entitlement to authority is built into our everyday usage of the term. Authority is also usually linked to right in philosophical analysis: David Bell, for example, claims that authority 'always implies a belief as to right'. This right may stem either from having special qualifications to speak authoritatively or from holding a social position or political office which bestows the right to give authoritative advice or to issue commands. It may, however, be urged, as it is by Richard B. Friedman in a very lucid and interesting essay, 'On the Concept of Authority in Political Philosophy', that these are two very different kinds of right relating to two distinct types of authority.

Two Types of Authority or One?

At this point it is necessary to clarify whether there are two quite separate social roles – being an authority and being in authority – which happen to share the same name, or whether there is a single phenomenon which can be identified as authority and which has different manifestations. The advantage of arguing that there are two types of authority is that it seems in many ways clearer and simpler. For example, when faced with two competing and plausible definitions of authority – that authority means to command a respectful hearing, the formula suggested by De Jouvenel in *The Pure Theory of Politics*, and that authority means to command obedience, which is the more usual formulation – it is possible to assign the first to being an authority and the second to being in authority. It is also possible to set out the different characteristics and conditions of each type of authority in a way which answers a number of vexed questions: whether the authority relationship necessarily implies superiority and subordination; whether acceptance of authority requires unthinking compliance; and whether obedience to authority must mean belief that the commands are inherently right. Closer examination, however, suggests that there is still room for dispute about how each type of authority should be characterized.

Richard Friedman produces one interpretation of how the two types of authority differ. He claims that the kind of authority which comes from superior knowledge is totally different in its nature from the kind of authority which is attained through holding political office. To recognize someone as an authority means to recognize inherent superiority, to give unquestioning assent and to believe that what authority says must be right. To recognize that someone is in authority implies no awareness of innate superiority, may involve critical assessment of authoritative statements and does not require belief in the rightness of each command, even though obedience is obligatory. The authority of knowledge is based on tradition; the authority of office is based on recognition of the necessity of office-holders and acceptance of the rules which select people for office.

The main objection to be made to Friedman's characterization of the two types of authority is that he appears to be superimposing one basic distinction – the contrast between authority derived from consensus on shared beliefs, which is typical of traditional society, and the authority stemming from a common framework of accepted rules, which is more typical of rationalist society – upon the distinction between being an authority and being in authority. The result is to confuse our current understanding of what is meant by being an authority by infusing the hierarchical and authoritarian associations of traditional society into the image of authority based on special knowledge or wisdom. There are contexts in which being an authority may have these connotations – for example if authority is claimed on the basis of divine revelation. But in general it is arguable that the kind of authority associated with special knowledge is intrinsically non-hierarchical and implies a freedom to ask questions or refuse compliance.

It is true that the professional authority of the expert over the layman dependent upon him can be exercised in an authoritarian manner, but it does not necessarily entail the total surrender of private judgment by the layman. The expert is often in the position of serving his client, who expects proof of the expert's skill. A layman is not obliged to accept professional authority uncritically or unconditionally; it is always possible to get an alternative professional opinion. Nor does the right to give authoritative advice always imply unquestioning acceptance of it by the recipient. Indeed if the authority of knowledge corresponds to the right to obtain a respectful hearing, and if an authority gives weighty advice rather than issuing commands, it does not imply a relationship between a superior and inferior, and authoritative utterances are not binding.

The professional speaking to those who have specialist knowledge in other fields is among equals. The architect will defer to the expertise of the engineer or town planner; the historian of Byzantine art will accept another's authority on Greek archaeology. This relationship is aptly described by Carl Friedrich as one of 'mutual authority'. Within a particular profession or craft some practitioners have greater authority than others: because of greater experience, greater knowledge in a particular area, or recognized exceptional skills. But the ground for this authority is not a hierarchy of experience or skill; it is rather a common understanding and skill which qualifies those sharing the mastery of the subject to recognize excellence and confer special authority. The authority of a leading philosopher or nuclear physicist is created by the judgment of his peers, since the uninitiated accept the special authority of an individual professional on the basis of the collective authority of those able to judge. It is only if external social considerations of pay, status, prestige and power intrude into professional relationships that any sort of hierarchy is imposed upon them.

The second objection to Friedman's thesis is that an attempt to differentiate sharply between an authority and being in authority ignores the extent to which the two are interrelated. Friedman limits his argument about the authority of office to politics. But it is not possible to limit the concept of being in authority to government, since it also applies to smaller-scale social organizations. There is an important sense too in which parents and teachers are in authority over children. In all these contexts being in authority is closely related to being an authority. Indeed if a pure authority – the right to voluntary compliance – can be isolated from the power of office or social status, then this authority must rest primarily on a claim to special qualifications. The adult status of parents, for example, and the professional status of teachers are, in a non-hierarchical society, justified only by greater experience and knowledge in relation to the child. Positions of authority at work are also related to a claim to special professional expertise, or to special administrative ability, or both. This is true, for example, of a head teacher, a matron, a ship's captain or a factory manager. These examples suggest that the right to be in authority is closely linked to the right to be an authority, and that attempts to maintain a clear distinction between the two types of authority are mistaken. (This question is discussed in more detail in the next chapter, which examines the nature of political authority.)

The view that authority is the antithesis of force and the claim that there is only one basic kind of authority are both reinforced if one looks for the essential meaning of authority in the historical origins of the concept: that is in the Roman idea of *auctoritas*. Since the Romans coined the word for the social and political phenomenon of authority and handed the word and the idea down to us, it is important to know what they meant by it. The meaning of *auctoritas* is not easily translated into contemporary terms, and is best understood within the political framework of republican Rome, where the *auctoritas* belonging to the Senate was contrasted with the *potestas* (power) belonging to the popular assembly. The Roman Senate did not have the right or the ability to command automatic obedience, but it could command a respectful hearing, and because its counsel was authoritative the popular assembly would normally do what the Senate urged. When Mommsen tried to define precisely the exact weight attaching to the counsel given by the Senate, he described it as 'more than advice and less than command'. Carl Friedrich seeks to translate this concept into modern terms by adding the gloss: 'It is advice which cannot be safely disregarded, such as the expert gives to the layman or a leader in parliament and party to his followers' (*Tradition and Authority*, p. 47). The idea of *auctoritas* had additional connotations, which are considered where appropriate below, but the main meaning is embodied in the Senate's relationship to the plebs.

There are difficulties involved in sticking too closely to the Roman understanding of *auctoritas*. If, as Hannah Arendt tends to suggest, the Romans enjoyed a unique and never to be fully repeated social and political experience of true authority, then the meaning of *auctoritas* is of primarily antiquarian interest. On the other hand if the concept is abstracted from its context and generalized, it is in danger of losing its real meaning. Nevertheless some degree of abstraction and generalization is necessary to apply it to a contemporary social context. *Auctoritas* implies the ability to command respect and voluntary compliance both by virtue of holding an authoritative position and by being qualified to give authoritative advice. This idea of authority can be transferred to the role of parent, which combines a social status with the qualifications of adult experience. The connexion was in fact made by the Romans, who often referred to the Senate as *patres* – it is important, however, to distinguish between the *auctoritas* of the parent and the absolute rule exercised by the father in Rome over his family. The idea of *auctoritas* can be translated fairly easily to the sphere of professional knowledge, as Friedrich indicates. In the political realm Hannah Arendt suggests that the nearest modern equivalent to the kind of authority embodied in the Roman Senate is the American Supreme Court, which interprets the Constitution inherited from the Founding Fathers in the light of contemporary problems, and which issues decisions which are authoritative and binding, but which cannot be enforced by the Court, so that the authority of the Court depends on the co-operation and voluntary compliance of the other branches of government.

The Problem of *de facto* Authority

One necessary element in *auctoritas* and in any form of authority is, as already noted, that it entails the right to be heard with respect and the right to prescribe what should be done or should be believed. Some definitions of authority, however, such as De Jouvenel's suggestion that authority means the ability to make oneself heard, stress effectiveness as a measure of authority rather than right. It is certainly arguable that authority does not exist unless it is effectively recognized. What is more puzzling is whether a natural or effective authority can exist without any socially recognized entitlement to it: whether in R. S. Peters's terms *de facto* authority can exist independent of *de jure* authority (Quinton, *Political Philosophy*, pp. 89–92).

De Jouvenel chooses as an example of the problem of gaining authority Mark Antony's speech to the Roman crowd after the assassination of Caesar. Brutus speaks first, secure in the advantages of his family name and his own reputation as an outstanding citizen and experienced orator. Brutus represents our normal understanding of what is meant by authority: the automatic right to a hearing and the prior assumption that what is said will be worthy of respect. But his own right to be heard in this context, where there is no fully institutionalized authority, is a right attaching to his reputation and not strictly *de jure*. Mark Antony, however, starts without even a tacit right to be heard – he has to persuade his countrymen to lend him their ears before he can influence them. Mark Antony has to assert a natural authority, or else 'coerce' the crowd into listening to him through his demagogic skill.

Many examples of natural authority come from situations of accident or emergency where the normally recognized authorities are not available, so individuals take charge and act as though they had authority. But natural authority can be seen most vividly when it is asserted in opposition to the existing hierarchy of society. William Faulkner provides an example of natural authority which goes against the grain of the surrounding society in his portrait of Lucas Beauchamp, the black man in a Mississippi town who refuses to know his place. Lucas is shown to have a personal authority which elicits unhesitating obedience. The boy narrator, who is white, immediately experiences this authority. He is ordered by Lucas to follow him (*Intruder in the Dust*, p. 8):

he could no more imagine himeself contradicting the man striding on ahead of him than he could his grandfather, not from any fear of nor even the threat of reprisal but because like his grandfather the man striding ahead of him was simply incapable of conceiving himself by a child contradicted and defied.

It is important here to make a general point: authority cannot intelligibly be understood as an attribute of personality except in a purely metaphorical sense. Authority has to be acknowledged by another person and so denotes a social relationship. Certain individuals may have authority in the sense of evoking voluntary obedience, but authority denotes a role rather than inherent character traits. In the special case of natural authority an authoritative role is accorded someone on the basis of character traits normally associated with the exercise of authority.

In unstructured or informal social contexts it is possible to regard personal authority as a kind of social status, conferred by the judgment of a group over a period of time – as Brutus was recognized as an outstanding citizen worthy of being listened to with respect – or conferred almost instantaneously – as in the case of someone who takes charge after an accident. Cases of extraordinary authority, like Lucas Beauchamp, are derived from the authority roles of the dominant society. Lucas simply behaves like an adult towards a child and ignores the social distinctions of colour. In any situation where authority must be won by successful assumption of the right to command and by proved effectiveness, authority still depends on implicit beliefs about what gives a right to be obeyed, which may include knowing what to do when others hesitate. Any attempt to distinguish rigidly between *de jure* and *de facto* authority is therefore misleading, since instances of apparent exercise of *de facto* authority are effective only as an extension of the cases of authority where there is a socially recognized entitlement to it. R. S. Peters after introducing the distinction between the *de jure* and *de facto* senses of authority ends by concluding that the *de facto* sense implies an indeterminate and embryonic sense of 'having a right' to be obeyed.

Since there is some apparent similarity between the idea of natural authority and Max Weber's well-known category of charisma, it is worth clarifying the difference. Charisma is, in Weber's typology, a source of extraordinary personal dominance when the normal authorities are no longer in control, or are in the process of being challenged. Charisma is, in its original sense, a gift of grace from God, and Weber uses the term to indicate superhuman qualities of heroism or saintliness which inspire personal devotion. It is in its purest sense a far cry from the more mundane qualities of self-assurance, certitude, sound judgment, objectivity or appearance of integrity associated with the exercise of everyday kinds of authority and therefore with usual forms of natural authority. It is very doubtful if charismatic authority, either in the original sense or in watered down versions of charisma, corresponds to what is meant by pure authority in this book. Some of the reasons for this discrepancy between the two notions are examined later in relation to the general difficulties concerning Weber's categories and the problems of identifying charismatic political leaders. But a central reason why charisma differs from the concept of authority being elaborated here is that the sort of relationship implied by charisma is intrinsically different from the kind of relationship implied by a pure authority. It is the precise nature of this relationship that we must now examine in more detail.

The Authority Relationship and Voluntary Compliance

Hannah Arendt raises sharply the question of how the authority relationship should be defined. She claims in her essay that 'Against the egalitarian order of persuasion stands the authoritarian order, which is always hierarchical' (*Between Past and Future*, p. 93). What creates authority is the hierarchy itself. This is in part a logical point: authority fails to make sense as a concept unless it is contrasted with equality, because there is no reason to accord extreme respect and voluntary obedience to one's equals. It is also a historical claim, that authority only existed in certain types of hierarchical society. Part of Arendt's essay is clearly based on the Burkean image of an aristocratic society which enshrines true authority. She is, however, concerned to distinguish true authority, which depends upon purely voluntary obedience, from the use of force, and therefore for the reasons given in the previous chapter she cannot consistently identify authority with the social hierarchy of aristocratic society. In fact she does not explicitly commit herself to the conservative understanding of what authority was. Instead she explores the quite different model arising from the Roman experience and illustrated most clearly by the status of the Roman Senate. Even if the Senate originally derived its authority in part from its aristocratic status, it is clearly nonsensical to describe the relationship between the Senate and the plebs as hierarchical. It was rather a relationship of dual inequality in which the Senate possessed greater prestige while the people possessed superior power. What emerges from an attempt to define the precise relationship indicated by authority is – as Arendt herself stresses – that we lack the concepts and vocabulary to delineate at all precisely the position occupied by authority. Just as Mommsen sought to define the weight attaching to the Senate's counsel by describing it as 'more than advice and less than command', so the status of the Senate cannot be fitted into our categories of equality and hierarchy. It is because authority does not rest on power relationships that we need a different perspective upon it.

However, several points can be made about the nature of the

authority relationship which distinguish it from pure subordination to a superior. The first is that authority is limited in its scope and is often grounded on temporary differences in knowledge and ability. Professional authority in relation to a layman is permanent but it is only relevant in strictly limited spheres. For example, a patient comes under the authority of a doctor only when ill. The authority of parents disappears when children grow up, the authority of teachers declines as their students become better informed, and subordinates at work may in due course replace their previous seniors. In all these spheres the authority relationship is based on commonly accessible knowledge and experience and is therefore distinct from the rigid and permanent social hierarchy of aristocratic society, in which parents were entitled to obedience for ever and in which the deference due to social superiors remained unchanging from cradle to grave.

More important than the limited and in some cases temporary nature of authority, however, is the quality of the authority relationship, and this can be clarified by examining what is meant by voluntary compliance. Obedience is clearly involuntary when it results from unwilling submission to physical coercion or threats of force. Therefore the obedience given to superiors in aristocratic society or in a bureaucratic organization that is based on fear of sanctions is not voluntary, even though the right to command may be fully acknowledged. On the other hand it is possible to comply willingly with commands — because of a sense of duty or through respect for office — while knowing that disobedience will be punished. In this case obedience may be voluntary in terms of the internal response of the person responding to orders, but it is not free, since free obedience implies the freedom to disobey. If voluntariness implies the ability to make a choice, then genuinely voluntary compliance must include the realistic possibility of disobedience, that is the freedom to disobey.

Aristocratic society may often have obtained willing obedience, but the obedience of children to their parents, peasants to their lords or subjects to their king was not free. There was no practical choice because obedience could be enforced. In addition it is arguable that there was no moral choice because there was normally (excluding circumstances of possible conflict between church and king) no possible justification within the dominant values of the society for disobedience. There is moreover an inherent incompatibility between a strictly hierarchical relationship and a relationship involving voluntary acceptance of authority. Voluntary consent to authority does not imply strict subordination to a superior, but the right and ability to withdraw consent under certain conditions.

The precise meaning of voluntary compliance is made ambiguous by the overlapping of hierarchical and non-hierarchical concepts of authority. The hierarchical image suggests that obedience should be unhesitating and unquestioning, and this also seems to follow from contrasting authority with persuasion which relies on reason and argument. When Faulkner's boy narrator recognizes the authority of Lucas Beauchamp he does so by obeying unhesitatingly. This example comes, of course, from a relatively hierarchical kind of society in which adults expected unquestioning obedience, and so borders on a relationship of automatic submission to social superiors. It is possible to imagine situations in an egalitarian context in which following authoritative advice would be very close to allowing oneself to be persuaded. Voluntary compliance can best be understood therefore in terms of a spectrum, with unhesitating obedience at one end and considered acceptance of authoritative counsel at the other, and it is easiest to characterize the authority relationship in terms of an automatic *tendency* to comply.

It is misleading to assume that unhesitating obedience necessarily implies unquestioning obedience, because there are occasions when the decision to obey may be considered but almost instantaneous. The speed with which people obey authority depends not only on the degree of respect but also on the context: in an emergency people naturally respond rapidly even to an *ad hoc* authority whereas some forms of professional advice invite reflection. It is totally unquestioning obedience, which involves abdication of the right and the ability to choose to disobey, that is incompatible with a pure authority relationship.

If obedience is blind and unconditional it is doubtful whether it remains truly voluntary. For example in the Stanley Milgram experiment, in which volunteers obeyed orders to give electric shocks to people even when they believed the shocks caused great pain or might be lethal, often the volunteers obeyed despite feelings of doubt and distress. Some of the volunteers obeyed against their better judgment and in a sense against their will. Far from being an example of 'obedience to authority' in the specialized sense authority is being defined here, this experiment was rather an example of involuntary submission to orders from above, even though there were no external constraints or sanctions or binding obligations upon the participants. It therefore appears that people may be induced to give involuntary obedience to commands without the use of any kind of physical or legal coercion, but by purely psychological means.

Obedience which is involuntary in a purely psychological sense may be psychologically forced. The parallel between psychological or spiritual force and force in the social sphere is drawn by Thomas Mann in his story of Mario and the Magician. The hypnotic power of the magician symbolizes the impact of the growing power of fascism in Italy, and its assault on both the mind and the will. In the story the gentleman from Rome does not want to dance and resists the magician's command until he is deprived of his will to resist. Mann's narrator observes that it was the subduing of the rebellious spirit of the young

Roman that set the seal on the hypnotist's supremacy (*Stories of a Lifetime*, vol. 2, p. 204):

> For now he made them dance, yes, literally; and the dancing lent a dissolute, abandoned, topsy-turvy air to the scene, a drunken abdication of the critical spirit which had so long resisted the spell of this man.

Mann's story suggests one reason why authority should be distinguished from Weber's category of charisma. As charisma suggests supernatural spiritual power and influence, it is much more akin to the hypnotic influence of the magician than it is to the ability to evoke a sober and reasoned acceptance of the authoritativeness of a command. Charisma may conjure up a devotion and obedience which is irrational, or even contrary to reason. Genuinely voluntary compliance involves an element of rational consideration.

Personal magnetism or hypnotic force of personality are extraordinary causes of blind and unconditional obedience to commands. There are three more common and more rational grounds for unquestioning obedience: the habit of accepting orders from above; complete trust in the person giving the orders; or awareness of one's own inability to judge whether what is commanded is correct. The habit of obeying orders unthinkingly may be inculcated by a hierarchical society which promotes automatic social deference, or by a hierarchical organization which sets a premium on obedience to superiors, and in both cases habit may lead to blind obedience. The participants in the experiment described by Milgram were presumably in the habit of obeying orders from superiors. Nevertheless a degree of habit, that is a customary predisposition to obey, seems to be a necessary condition for the existence of authority. Similarly blind trust is incompatible with voluntary acceptance of specific orders, since it rules out the possibility of disobedience; yet trust is a necessary condition of accepting authority, as is an awareness of one's own ignorance.

Reason and Authority

In order to discover how the necessity of habit and trust to the existence of authority can be squared with the necessity of a questioning and rational attitude in relation to authority, it is useful to examine the thesis put forward by Carl Friedrich. Friedrich gives priority in his definition of authority to the importance of reasoned acceptance of authoritative pronouncements. He claims that the existence of good reasons for a decision or command is the basis of authority, rather than the prestige of the person or body issuing the orders. Thus the grounds for the willing obedience accorded to true authority lie in the intrinsic reasonableness and validity of the commands. He does stress that authority is characterized by the potentiality of reasoned elaboration – implying the reasons are often taken on trust – but implies also the potentiality of critical assessment of the reasons if given.

Whereas most writers on authority take it for granted that authority resides in the person or office responsible for issuing commands or judgments, Friedrich looks not to the source of the communication but to the communication itself. 'It is the communication rather than the communicator that is in a strict sense possessed of authority' (*Tradition and Authority*, p. 54). He illustrates this statement by suggesting that: 'Reason and experience as embodied in a judicial decision give it authority and through its writing the judge acquires authority'. This statement fails to explain the authority inherent in the position of a judge, which does not rest primarily on specific judgments but on the judge's role in interpreting the law. Friedrich, in his anxiety to show that 'authority is not an alternative to reason but is grounded in it' (p. 55), has telescoped two distinct levels of authority that require different forms of reasoned elaboration.

One level of authority concerns the specific orders or judgments issued by those who have authority. At this level we often expect reasoned elaboration of particular decisions, as in the case of judicial decisions. Even if the order or advice is accepted on trust, this trust is based on the assumption that sound reasons could be given if required.

The second level concerns the validity of a particular form of authority *per se*. If we ask why an institution like a court is entitled to issue authoritative judgments, the kind of answer we receive will be a different kind of reasoned justification from the answer we receive if we ask if a particular judgment was correct. In the latter case the answer operates within the agreed criteria of legal decisions. In the former we are questioning the validity of a legal tradition. If we are simply seeking clarification we may be satisfied by various possible answers, whether they appeal to custom and history, or to the constitution, or to the general necessity of law and legal institutions in all societies. But if we press our questions to the point of radical scepticism then our demand for reasons is incompatible with acceptance of authority. Unless there is a fairly widespread and unquestioning acceptance of the figure or body in authority, the foundations of authority are being undermined.

At this point it is possible to reconcile the requirements that authority should be based on a habit of obedience and on unquestioning trust and that recognition of authority – as opposed to submission to power – depends on the exercise of critical judgment. Authority must be defined primarily in terms of roles which are recognised as authoritative within a given community. The role may be political – a senator or judge; social – a father or priest; or professional – a teacher or doctor. The exercise of authority normally depends on a clearly recognized entitlement to it. To have authority in this sense is to have an automatic right to be heard and to be able to invoke an automatic tendency to comply with one's advice or commands.

It is necessary however to distinguish between the roles of authority and specific persons in authority, their decisions and their performance. It is here that a degree of critical evaluation and a desire to make those who exercise authority accountable for their decisions is appropriate, if authority is to be maintained. An automatic respect for the judiciary is quite compatible, within certain limits, with criticizing individual judges or specific decisions. Indeed that aspect of authority which lies, in Friedrich's phrase, in the quality of communication, is an essential complement to the authority that resides in the prestige of persons or offices. A judge who frequently hands down bad judgments has relinquished his original qualification to be listened to with automatic respect. He has lost the living quality of authority although he may keep his position. Without some degree of critical evaluation by other bodies or the public no institution or individual can maintain real authority as opposed to unthinking acceptance. There must be a large element of habit in the response to authority, but blind habit may overlook the irrationality of judgments or the misuse of institutions, and by condoning false or meaningless assertions of authority encourage a new generation to overthrow it altogether. There is therefore no necessary incompatibility in saying that authority requires unquestioning trust and that its exercise must be based on good reasons.

There is a spectrum of authority, with natural authority embodying the living quality of authority at one end and the authority embodied in institutional offices at the other. The argument of this chapter leads to the conclusion that authority must imply at least an embryonic role and permanent authority depends on permanent authority roles. On the other hand the validity of authority also depends on individuals living up to their positions; the obverse of this requirement is a public who accord voluntary compliance but not blind obedience. De Jouvenel in *The Pure Theory of Politics* suggests that the institutions of official authority and the dynamic process of authority as exercised in day to day life are distinct concepts, requiring separate names, whereas it is maintained here that they are necessarily complementary.

Chapter 3
The Nature of Political Authority

Political authority, it is often argued, poses particular problems in any general analysis of this topic. One central question posed by political authority is whether it is simply an extension of other forms of authority or whether it rests on quite separate bases and is different in nature. An exploration of the sources of political authority involves consideration of Weber's much cited classification of three general types of 'authority', of the nature of representation and of the relevance of Hobbes's theory of authorization. If political authority rests on grounds which are distinct from the grounds of other kinds of authority it does not necessarily follow that political authority is totally different from other modes of social authority. This chapter discusses three issues which bear on this problem: the nature of voluntary consent to political authority; whether assent to political authority means assenting to the rightness of all authoritative decisions or commands; and how far it is possible to compare political and professional authority. The chapter concludes with a brief examination of the nature of political authority and its relation to direct democracy.

Weber's Typology

It is impossible to explore the meaning of political authority in the past and present without considering Weber's three pure types of 'authority': traditional, rational–legal and charismatic. Weber's typology is related to modes of social action and of the social relationships characteristic of different kinds of society, and therefore subsumes political command under a broader category of 'authority', but is generally seen as especially relevant to political authority. It is however debatable whether Weber's categories do resolve the problems surrounding the nature of political authority.

The first issue to be clarified concerns the meaning of Weber's term

26

'*legitime Herrschaft*', which is translated by Talcott Parsons and usually interpreted as 'authority', but which is translated by both Reinhard Bendix and Raymond Aron with greater plausibility as 'legitimate domination'. (For a more detailed discussion of the problems of translating *Herrschaft* and difficulties with Weber's categories see: Dennis Wrong (ed.), *Max Weber*, in particular the Introduction by Wrong and the essay by Peter Blau 'Critical Remarks on Weber's Theory of Authority'.) By '*Herrschaft*' Weber means the ability of a leader to command the obedience of a group. It is distinguished from '*Macht*' which covers any means whereby one person imposes his will upon another. Weber specifies that a criterion of every true relationship involving *Herrschaft* is 'a certain minimum of voluntary submission'. He also suggests that the most important factor promoting the stability of *Herrschaft* is belief in legitimacy. But the concept of *legitime Herrschaft* does include, as Weber makes clear, ability to impose discipline and use coercive sanctions. It is a form of rule rather than a form of pure authority as defined in the previous chapter, though rule should be understood in a social as well as a political sense.

Weber's categories are, as he stresses, abstract types not descriptions of concrete reality. Since charisma is in its nature an extraordinary and temporary phenomenon disrupting established social patterns, the two main types of legitimate rule are traditional and rational–legal rule. Traditional rule according to Weber means a social order based on immemorial custom in which status and the rights of the leader are also defined by custom. Traditional rule also entails an element of personal loyalty linking men to their lord and a degree of personal arbitrariness in the way the lord assigns office and favour. Weber's category of traditional society of course comprises aristocratic society, but it is very much broader since it covers the whole range of historically known societies based on custom, and its primary models are patriarchal rule over a household and the extension of patriarchal rule to patrimonial government, based on the absolute personal control of the ruler over his subjects and domains. Weber's category of traditional society, unlike the ideal type elaborated by Nisbet, does not stress either hierarchy or limits on the sphere of authoritative control. It is defined rather by qualities which are in direct contrast to the rational–legal type of social order: unwritten custom, personal arbitrariness and personal attachment. In the rational–legal type all the rules are written down and clearly stated, the sphere of each official's competence is defined by the rules and obedience is owed not to persons but to an impersonal office. The purest model of rational–legal order is bureaucratic organization, which implies a strict hierarchy and strict rules controlling office holders. The individual is selected for bureaucratic office in terms of general requirements of competence, he enters office through a free contractual relationship, and is dependent for promotion on his superiors.

Several difficulties arise when one attempts to fit representative and constitutional government into Weber's typology. It is often assumed that representative institutions are an aspect of rational–legal order. There appear to be two reasons for this belief: the modern state typifies the rational–legal mode of social organization which has supplanted traditionalism and therefore the characteristic form of government in Western bureaucratic society is assimilated to the rational–legal order; and Weber's own summary of what is meant by rationalist legitimacy – 'belief in the "legality" of patterns of normative rules and the right of those elected to authority under such rules to issue commands' (*Theory of Economic and Social Organization*, p. 328) – as well as parts of his more extended examination of this form of rule does seem to allow for elected officials as well as bureaucats. On the other hand there is also a good deal of evidence in Weber's discussion of *legitime Herrschaft* that he sees electoral democracy primarily as an aspect of the routinization of charisma. He suggests that the origin of election lies in the designation of a successor by a charismatically qualified leader (p. 365), and examines in some detail how plebiscites and elections may provide democratic legitimacy for a type of charismatic leadership (pp. 386–92). It is also arguable, and rather indirectly suggested by Weber in his treatment of traditional rule, that the historical evolution of constitutional and representative government has meant that in practice the legitimacy of parliamentary democracy depends a good deal on historical continuity and on the values and attitudes associated with a traditional social order.

The fact that elements of all three types of legitimate rule may be found in representative government does not in itself create insuperable problems. Weber emphasizes that the pure types of rule hardly ever exist and that tradition may supplement law (p. 328). But it should be possible to show that representative government does belong predominantly to one type, if it is to be fitted into Weber's threefold category; and it is not.

Representation cannot plausibly be seen as a form of traditional legitimacy, since neither custom nor personal loyalty are the primary constituent of representation; and although representative democracy may allow for the exercise of charisma, the legitimacy of representation is certainly not based on charisma. It does not make sense either to see representation primarily as a form of rational–legal rule as Weber defines this category. Weber himself suggests that bureaucracy, which is the purest type of legal rule, is characterized by the principle of appointment and so is inherently in conflict with the principle of election. It is as unsatisfactory to graft representative government on to a bureaucratic hierarchy as an extension of the same kind of rule as it is to see representative government as an extension of the social hierarchy of aristocratic society. The legitimacy of a representative leader does not stem from being either chief administrator or chief patriarch. Representation logically entails a quite separate basis for legitimacy stemming from the consent of the people.

Weber shows his awareness of the importance of representation and of constitutional limits on government power in any comprehensive theory of the bases of legitimate rule by including chapters on both these topics in the overall section on types of legitimacy. It is not clear how he interprets their significance. He does indicate that both are compatible with either traditional or legal forms of rule: his examples of separation of powers and representation are drawn from both traditional and modern types of society. But the categories of traditionalism and rationalism are being used here very much more loosely than in the specification of the pure types, and refer to actual historical periods (pp. 392–407 and 412–23).

One very interesting point is made by Weber when he is characterizing representative legitimacy. He introduces his discussion by commenting that some corporate groups try to minimize the element of *Herrschaft*, and require their leaders to act 'solely in accordance with the will of their members' (p. 412). After itemizing types of direct democracy he outlines different historical examples of representation. Weber is therefore explicitly departing from the authoritarian nature of the traditional and legal types of legitimate domination and seems to be suggesting a type of polity which minimizes coercion and maximizes reliance on voluntary consent. It is the nearest Weber comes to speaking of a pure authority distinct from coercion; but since he is still concentrating on a form of rule and since the relevance of representation is not clearly related to his basic threefold scheme of types of legitimacy, he cannot take us any further in exploring the nature of political authority.

Representation and Authorization

There are two main strands in the theory underlying representative authority: the right to act and speak for the body politic, a right which stems from holding office that symbolizes the political realm; and a right to represent the nation, which flows from election from below. This understanding of representative authority, which has evolved historically from the feudal period, was originally centred on the person of the monarch but extended to parliament.

In the early medieval period the king was sometimes portrayed as being Christ's representative on earth. Later the pope claimed exclusive title to represent Christ, but the distinction which had been drawn between the king in his personal capacity and the king in his divine capacity acquired secular political connotations. The immortal personality of the king came to represent the realm he governed and its continuity. By the time of Queen Elizabeth I an elaborate distinction between the king's two bodies, his natural body and the body politic, was used as part of English legal argument in cases touching the monarch.

The monarch represented the realm most obviously in relation to other rulers, but an essential aspect of the claim to kingly authority was that in relation to his subjects he represented and visibly maintained the commonweal. The representative authority of the English king extended by the time of Henry VIII to 'the king in parliament', which became the source of legislation affecting the nation and the symbol of that nation. The distinction between the individual king and the institution of kingship, and the actual symbol of the 'king in parliament', were both used by the puritans and parliamentarians in the Civil War. The puritans could cry, 'We fight the king to defend the king', and Parliament could claim in 1642 that what Parliament did 'had the stamp of Royal Authority, although His Majesty ... do in his own Person oppose or interrupt the same' (quoted by Kantorowicz in *The King's Two Bodies*, p. 21). Theories appealing to the customary limits to the king's power and to the historic rights of the people of the realm were also stressed and could find some kind of historical warrant, but the evolution of parliamentary representation had been closely tied to the representative status of the king.

Voegelin comments that at the time of Magna Carta Parliament was still only the 'common council of our realm', while the king remained sole representative of the realm of England (*The New Science of Politics*, p. 38). Parliaments only gradually acquired their own independent representative status. The first step towards representation was for the ad hoc consultative assemblies called by the king to differentiate themselves into estates and chambers, so that the various orders and corporations found themselves a representative voice in these assemblies. Representation required a degree of social articulation, and the representative principle was most highly developed in the church, especially among certain monastic orders. Like the clergy, the higher and lower nobility, and the towns began to see themselves as part of a unified body: the realm, country, people or kingdom. Marongui in his comparative study of medieval parliaments suggests that 'to convoke parliament meant to convoke the kingdom'. He illustrates this by citing the terms used for the Spanish parliaments – for instance a new session of the Castilian *cortes* was known as 'another kingdom' (*Medieval Parliaments*, p. 244).

Parliament as it evolved could sometimes be used to express the resistance of the feudal magnates to the king and to affirm the necessity of limiting royal power; Simon de Montfort's parliament of 1265 is an instance of this parliamentary role. However, the prevailing idea of parliament did not endow it with independent authority against the king, but rather saw it as an extension and complement of the king's representative authority until well after the medieval period. In England the struggle between crown and parliament, which began under Queen Elizabeth and led to war under the Stuarts, was not finally resolved in favour of parliament until 1688. The Convention Parliament which conferred the crown on William and Mary claimed to be, as the House of Lords declared, 'a full and free representative of this Nation (McIlwain, *Constitutionalism*, p. 5). The aspect of representative authority which flows from election from below has become increasingly significant in modern representative institutions with the extension of the franchise and spread of democratic ideas and attitudes, though it does not exclude the symbolic element in all forms of representation.

Closely intertwined with the concept of representation is that of delegated authority. Delegation in turn implies authorization, a word which has close associations with the concept of authority and includes one of the connotations of *auctoritas*, the idea of authorship or originating action. Hobbes deals with the link between authority and authorization in the *Leviathan* as follows:

> Of persons artificial, some have felt their words and actions *owned* by those whome they represent. And then the person is the *actor*; and he that owneth his words and actions, is the AUTHOR: in which case the actor acteth by authority ... So that by authority, is always understood a right of doing any act; and *done by authority*, done by commission, or license from him whose right it is (p. 125).

Hobbes introduces the notion of authorization to prove that all actions taken on the initiative of the sovereign have been authorized by the people through the original contract and they are not therefore entitled to complain at what the sovereign does. In this passage Hobbes is playing with the ideas of representation and authorization, ideas which belonged most naturally to the parliamentarians, in order to prove the case for autocratic rule and to deny the logical possibility of a right to rebellion. Hobbes's formal conception implies that the person who has been authorized to act is not so much a representative, in the usual sense of the word, but a delegate of those he is acting for. If the abstract conception of the social contract is translated into actual vesting of powers in a person by some electoral body, then authorization to act in the name of the electorate implies a limited and revocable delegation of the right to act. So Hobbes's justification of absolute sovereignty can be turned on its head to provide a justification for the most extreme form of populist democracy.

The kind of authority created by the process of authorization is quite distinct from the kind of authority being analysed in this book, because the person who is authorized to act is in a strictly subordinate position to the author, who retains a supreme right of command and decision. Similarly delegation is in principle quite distinct from representation, and the delegate has political authority only in the sense of having been authorized, not in the sense of having a right to make decisions or issue commands or being able to evoke an automatic tendency to respect.

Representation is necessary to the existence of political authority, but it is not sufficient. It is generally agreed by political theorists of authority that it depends also on two other requirements, usually associated with constitutionalism: limitation on the power of government and the political freedom of citizens. It has already been argued that authority by definition implies limits on its sphere of operation, and the distinction between authority and absolute power in the political realm is elaborated in the discussion of sovereignty. What is central here is how far the freedom available in constitutional régimes and the nature of the representative process affect the kind of voluntary consent accorded to consitutional governments.

Is Consent to Political Authority Voluntary?

There is certainly one sense in which constitutional and representative governments do appear to rest on free consent to a greater extent than less free kinds of government. There is also a sense in which they invite a reasoned and critical compliance with governmental commands. The citizens in a constitutional state are free to criticize openly the nature of governmental decisions, to propose alternatives and to take forms of constitutionally recognized action to change laws and policies. In addition citizens under a representative government have a periodic opportunity of voting to select a new government if they opposed the actions of the existing government. Their obligation to obey the government is therefore neither unconditional nor unquestioning – on the contrary, the exercise of political freedom presupposes the right to make constant assessments and to question political decisions. In this sense citizens accord constitutional governments a reasoned compliance.

There is, however, another sense in which citizens of constitutional states appear less morally free to disobey their government than the subjects of despotic régimes. It is often argued that precisely because they enjoy a freedom of criticism and political action, as well as a chance to alter their government, they are morally bound to obey the law and the government. So from one perspective it could be argued that the citizens in a constitutional state have lost the moral right to choose to disobey, and that their obedience is in this sense more involuntary than that accorded to tyrannical governments, where the moral right of disobedience exists if one is prepared to risk the physical consequences. The relevance of this line of argument depends somewhat on the effectiveness of the political freedoms and forms of constitutional action open to citizens, but it remains true that minorities may be permanently obliged to accept commands they believe to be wrong.

The degree of voluntariness in the consent accorded to political authority can be maximized if the prevailing political beliefs allow for the right of rebellion if government steps outside the constitutionally set limits, where the areas of individual dissent that are tolerated are stretched to include forms of conscientious objection to government policies, and where a moral right to civil disobedience is accepted even when it remains legally punishable. Even a constitutional government acting with great liberalism and tolerance cannot rest on pure authority, since it relies ultimately on coercion; it can only claim to embody a greater clement of authority than any other government.

It is, however, debatable whether the voluntary consent accorded to political authority must imply consent to every individual law passed and decision made; or to rephrase the same point, it is debatable whether recognition of political authority entails belief in the intrinsic rightness of each decision, or only belief that the right to make decisions and to command is inherent in political office, as Richard Friedman suggests. If this latter position is stated in extreme terms – that acceptance of the right to command involves unconditional obedience whatever the nature of the orders – then it is necessarily incompatible with the basic idea of authority presented in this book and it represents an unusually rigorous interpretation of political obligation. If this position is stated more moderately – that acceptance of the right to command involves a commitment to obey most orders in most circumstances even if one doubts their wisdom – it is persuasive. Respect for political office and a disposition to obey must be a primary element in political authority. There is moreover almost certainly a zone of indifference, in which people obey because they believe they should without having any strong views on the content of the order. They may even acquiesce in policies they believe are positively ill-judged because they accept the authority of office and the necessity of such authority for the sake of public order. The rightness of specific commands is therefore arguably a secondary factor in acceptance of political authority up to the point where the commands seem so clearly wrong or dangerous that consent is withdrawn. But if this much is granted to Friedman's case, it does not concede the core of his argument – that judgments of the rightness of specific commands are irrelevant to political authority – since it is being maintained that the rightness of commands remains a relevant, though not in many circumstances an overriding consideration, when giving voluntary obedience.

This account of the nature of voluntary consent given to political authority suggests that political authority is not different in kind from other forms of authority, which involve respect for the authority role, recognition of the right to give judgments or orders, and a habitual tendency to comply. The difference lies in the scope of the political sphere, the greater importance of decisions and the possibility of greater disasters arising either from mistaken obedience or from massive disobedience.

If the authority of a political office cannot be upheld wholly regardless of the decisions taken, it also depends – as suggested in the last chapter – on the quality of the office holder. Friedman's analysis of what is meant by being in authority concludes that authority derives only from agreement about the validity of rules of procedure, and that these rules are necessary precisely because office holders have no claim to inherent and permanent superiority. This claim that people respect the office rather than the person holding it clearly has an element of truth in any relatively democratic context: to take a simple example, people normally fall silent for the chairman of a meeting. But to maintain control of any lively meeting requires both tactical skill and the assertion of a more purely personal authority. So although respect for office is necessary it is not enough, and the authority of office is not sufficient to gain voluntary compliance with specific decisions from a group of one's peers. It is also arguable that the very nature of elections – the typical process for filling political office in a democratic society – entails choice of those with good qualifications for office. Electing someone need not imply any belief in his or her inherent superiority, but it does usually imply belief in competence and so the right, which stems from being qualified, of the specific individual to hold that office. There is a sense in which political offices which are more remote can rely more on a general and abstract respect for office divorced from assessment of the individual performance, but it is doubtful whether such generalized respect will by itself prevail over political interests or passions which are opposed to the commands of authority. Friedman's theory of political authority draws explicitly on Hobbes, and the kind of political authority he envisages rests only on the obligations of the social contract without any social or psychological support.

Friedman's concept of political authority is devised to account for voluntary consent in circumstances where there is no automatic unity of belief and no tradition to which authority can appeal. Where there is such a tradition he is prepared to accept that an elder or king or pope holding political office may be revered as an authority with special knowledge and ability. The point which is being made here is that there is a general social tendency to associate the right to be in authority with the right to be an authority, and that this applies, even though in an attenuated form, in democratic politics.

Professionalism in Politics

If authority is dependent not only upon respect for political office but for the quality and skills of the person occupying it, then there are two main reasons why politicians might be accorded special respect: social deference to the ruling class carried over from aristocratic society; or professional political expertise.

There is some historical evidence which seems to suggest that political authority may, even in a republican context, be strengthened by the habit of deference associated with an aristocratic order. The Roman acceptance of the authority of the Senate depended in part upon the aristocratic prestige of its members. Constitutional authority in Britain is historically connected with an aristocratic society, and the respect accorded Parliament has been reinforced by the social deference accorded to the class of men who went into the Commons as well as the Lords, as maintained not only by Burke but by Bagehot.

On the other hand even in these two cases what promoted the continuance of political authority was respect for political professionalism. The prestige of the Senate survived in a republican setting because it represented an aristocracy of proved talent and experience, and Burke's justification of the aristocracy's political role was their training as a class for political office and their education into the conventions and etiquette of civilized political activity.

The British parliamentary experience and unusual political stability might suggest that political authority is best preserved when democracy is still tempered by aristocratic values. There are, however, three reasons why social deference is wholly inadequate as a basis for representative authority. The first is that once representative status is based on wide or universal suffrage the logic of representation suggests the right of all social classes to be directly represented. The second is that the social deference tends to promote uncritical acceptance of unlimited power rather than qualified respect for limited authority, so there is a logical connexion between the deference shown to the British Parliament and its claims to unbounded sovereignty and its unwillingness to accept the views of the electorate on specific policies. The third is that once aristocratic values become obsolete, political authority which rests on social status and appeals to deference also becomes obsolete, and will be judged – probably harshly – by the criterion of political expertise.

It is in democratic societies no longer guided by tradition that professional models for political authority have most appeal, and it was the Greeks, who had no word for authority, who used analogies from the spheres of skill and knowledge to explain the special qualifications required to govern.

Plato's most famous attempt to resolve the two problems of creating good and stable government is expounded in *The Republic*, in which he appeals to a non-political concept of authority to create authority in the political sphere. The form of authority Plato invokes is that which flows from wisdom, but a special kind of wisdom which would, given Plato's theory of philosophy, be unchallengeable. The authority of the philosopher arises from an esoteric knowledge that must be accepted on trust by the common man. The authority of the true philosopher is then transferred to the political realm, where philosophers become kings, or the advisers of kings.

A more frequent analogy for political authority in Platonic dialogues is the analogy from the authority of the craftsman or expert in his given skill. In relation to the art of politics the analogy operates at two levels: to suggest the need for specialized skill in ruling comparable to the skill of the shoemaker or builder, and to suggest that the end of politics should be the good of those subject to the skill of the specialist. In *The Republic* Plato makes a comparison with the doctor and his patients and the shepherd and his flock to argue that the ruler's aim must be not crude self-interest but the interest of those under his care. He also uses in *The Republic* the comparison with a ship:

> The sailors are quarrelling over the control of the helm; each thinks he ought to be steering the vessel, though he has never learnt navigation and cannot point to any teacher under whom he has served apprenticeship; what is more, they assert that navigation is a thing that cannot be taught at all (p.191).

Because the captain of a ship exercises a dual skill – that of navigation and that of maintaining order among the crew – the image of the ship of state seems so appropriate that it has passed into cliché.

Hannah Arendt sees a danger in trying to transfer models drawn from the spheres of knowledge or of the crafts to politics, because the former easily becomes perverted into ideological indoctrination and the latter tends to transfer the violence which is involved in making and shaping material things into the political realm. Both these fears are justified, but they apply primarily to the special circumstances of the attempt to create a new society through revolution, discussed in chapter five, and there are contexts in which the idea of professionalism in politics is valid.

It is possible to pursue the analogy of professional authority in politics in two different contexts: the professional authority recognized by one's peers and the professional authority recognized by laymen. A political assembly is rather similar to a professional community: all in the assembly have an understanding of the craft of politics and can assess the skills of others, so that the masters of the craft are judged by an assembly of their fellows. The authority of the individual depends on the soundness of his advice and the effectiveness of his policies, which are subject to continual critical evaluation. This kind of analogy between politics and professional expertise does not have the authoritarian overtones of Plato's analogies in *The Republic*.

There are two objections to pressing this analogy too far. One is that the nature of knowledge and skill in politics is quite distinct from professional knowledge, and this difference affects the nature and stability of authority in each sphere. The authority of an established professional man is normally more or less permanent once established. The individual political expert may lose authority more through bad luck than bad judgment, or because the nature and beliefs of a democratic assembly change and they reject his advice. A form of political authority which relies solely on personal pre-eminence is therefore unstable and cannot guarantee continuity – Periclean Athens did not survive long without Pericles. Another objection is that purely personal authority within a democratic assembly is vulnerable to democratic pressures to deny any individual a permanent pre-eminence. One of the devices of classical Greek democracy was to ostracize some of its most talented and influential citizens and so exclude them from further political influence.

A rigidly egalitarian interpretation of democracy in the political sphere is opposed to the nature of learning and craftmanship which demands criteria of excellence.

The alternative model of professional authority in politics, which stresses the gulf between professional and layman, is potentially objectionable if interpreted in an authoritarian manner. It is a model which has been adopted by some contemporary élitist theorists of democracy like Schumpeter, who assumes an inevitable gulf between the politically initiated and the politically ignorant masses. The latter are obliged in the modern nation state to elect their representatives and then leave the esoteric business of government to them.

One question which arises out of the debate between élitists and democrats – and both the debate and the question go back to classical Greece – is whether there is a special kind of political skill that is only enjoyed by a minority, like the skill of mathematicians or composers. One answer is that while some people undoubtedly have more natural aptitude for political activity than others, the exercise of political judgment and political power is in principle accessible to anyone, resting as it does to a large degree on common experience and commonsense. It is also, of course, demonstrable that like any skill political ability improves with training; and training in politics consists in taking part in political activity and observing those more experienced. The argument for political participation has, since John Stuart Mill, rested in part on the claim that widespread involvement in politics will provide a political education that will among other things enable the electorate to assess the performance of the professional politicians.

If political skill is seen as necessarily related to experience and the opportunity to acquire knowledge, then in any centralized and specialized society some people will have greater understanding of particular political problems and greater expertise as political actors in specific contexts. On the other hand it can then be argued that it becomes more necessary for those who will be most affected by specialized decisions to take a more generalized look at the consequences for society as a whole. Aristotle's challenge to Plato, in which he claimed that although an individual layman may be a worse judge than an expert, an assembly of laymen may be better judges, and that in a number of arts the user is a better judge than the artist, is still relevant (*The Politics*, pp. 145–7). A democratic approach to modern politics suggests that there is a professional authority which should be respected in politics, both of purely professional expertise as of nuclear scientists or economists, and of political experience and knowledge in particular fields; but that political authority should still ultimately be judged by the political community which acknowledges that authority.

The Nature of Authority and Direct Democracy

At this point it is relevant to raise questions about the relationship between political authority and the ideal of direct democracy. If this ideal is carried to its logical conclusion it is necessarily in conflict with the theory of representation. The principles of direct democracy demand that decisions either be made directly by the group or, if it is essential to elect spokesmen, that representation should be replaced by delegation. A delegate is subject to constant recall and is accountable for the accuracy with which he follows instructions, not for the intrinsic soundness of his judgment or his independent contribution to the public good.

The only authority which can exist in a direct democracy is the collective 'authority' vested in the body politic. No individual can claim special authority, but it is arguable that the collectivity exercises the authority of all over each individual member. There are however reasons to query whether collective decisions are authoritative in the sense of demanding either a very special respect for the body making the decision or respect for the weight attaching to the decision. It is true a member of a democracy usually feels bound by collective decisions in taking action and accepts the validity of an agreed decision. But this sense of obligation and acceptance stems from a sense of the requirements of group membership and commitment to the validity of the democratic process, not from a belief in a collective authority. It is doubtful if authority can be created by a group of equals who reach decisions by a process of mutual persuasion. An individual has no good reason to ascribe superior collective wisdom to a group composed of his equals: and he is either persuaded that the final decision is right or he accepts a majority decision. There is of course a case that collective judgments are often better than individual judgments because different ideas and perspectives are pooled, but this is not an argument for the intrinsic or necessary superiority of group decisions. Indeed the tendency of democratic groups to reverse their own collective decisions, sometimes very rapidly, suggests the supremacy of the immediate popular will over the rightness of previous collective decisions. Because pure democracy seems incompatible with attempts to bind the collective, will, it is usually seen as incompatible with constitutional limits on popular decision making. The potential changeableness of the popular will in a pure democracy also appears incompatible with maintaining any constant political standards of right and wrong and with promoting social stability: two functions associated with constitutional or representative forms of authority.

The association between direct democracy and authority is promoted by Rousseau in his theory of the General Will. Because the image of the classical republic is central to *The Social Contract*, Rousseau can be interpreted as a theorist of direct democracy, denying the existence of any authority above or independent of the collective will of the assembled citizens, and specifically denouncing the idea of representation. But because he also asserts that the General Will cannot be limited and cannot bind itself, Rousseau links the popular will to a Hobbesian conception of unlimited sovereignty. If the popular will is endowed with a mythical and absolute superiority not susceptible to reasoned explanation, and if it is linked to the claim to overriding sovereign power, then the way is open to the manipulation of Rousseau's concept in the interests of repression.

Despite these contradictions in Rousseau's formulation of the General Will, it is possible to understand the General Will as a statement about the nature of political authority. It is implicit in the idea of political authority as embodied in a representative body that authority exists to promote the common good. The belief that authority vested in representative persons or offices should be exercised for the common good is built into the ceremonies for crowning kings, inaugurating presidents and summoning parliaments. Although Rousseau discards these institutions in his ideal state, he does associate the General Will by definition with the aim of the common good. The General Will can then be interpreted as a statement of the conditions necessary for the existence of political authority: that the institution which expresses the General Will ensures the respect and voluntary compliance of all citizens; that the General Will is necessarily directed to the common good of the political community; and that the process of decision-making by the authoritative body ensures that each decision comes as close to being objectively 'the right decision' as human fallibility allows. Rousseau poses a question at the heart of a debate about political authority: in what circumstances is it possible to achieve common acceptance of the law and at the same time ensure that the law is directed to the common good and worthy of voluntary obedience? In the ideal polity a pure form of authority could exist independent of the power of coercion.

The paradox of political authority lies in the fact that in those circumstances where voluntary acceptance of commonly agreed rules is most practicable, authority is also least necessary since the existence of common values and common interests should obviate major conflicts and create conditions favourable to direct democracy. Rousseau reflects this paradox. Where authority is most needed is where there are conflicts of basic interests and values, and the authority figure becomes responsible for promoting a central set of political values and taking the initiative to settle key conflicts or problems facing society. Thus the problem of authority is particularly crucial in the establishment of a new régime.

To sum up this examination of the sources and nature of political authority: it has been concluded that there is a distinctive source of political authority – the right of representation based on popular consent – but that political authority is not different in kind from other forms of authority inherent in social roles and drawing on various sources of knowledge and skill. Political authority, like other forms, entails a relationship of respect, an automatic tendency to comply with commands but a readiness to question the reasons for and the rightness of specific decisions.

Stable political authority must be embodied in political institutions, and acknowledgment of such authority is incompatible with the principle of direct democracy, if the latter is taken to its logical extremes of total egalitarianism and belief in the supremacy of the popular will. Finally, political authority rests on the assumption that it exists to promote the good of those who accept it, and is therefore incompatible with corrupt pursuit of self-interest by those in authority or use of force to coerce people into accepting involuntarily official definitions of the common good.

Chapter 4
Political Authority and Political Power

One major question which arises in any discussion of authority is the precise relationship between authority and the associated concepts of power, coercion and force. This question is relevant to the exercise of authority in all spheres of life, but is raised most acutely in the political sphere, where authority rarely exists in its pure form and where the exercise of authority is usually linked to the processes of government. It is also necessary at this point to distinguish between political authority, legitimacy and sovereignty.

Authority and Power

In the Roman definition of the words, political authority is clearly distinct from political power: in Cicero's phrase 'quum potestas in populo, auctoritas in senatu sit' ('power lies with the people, authority in the senate'). The Senate had authority because of its seniority, its aristocratic status, its experience in forms of government, and its resultant *dignitas* and *gravitas*. The people on the other hand had power because of their numbers, and because in the evolution of the Roman Republic they had won legal recognition of their right to power: a resolution passed by the assembly of plebeians was binding on the whole community.

The power of numbers consists in the potential for effective social action created by their participation in co-ordinated activity; it also can consist in the ability of a majority to overwhelm a minority. This twofold nature of power corresponds to common usage: the power to act or create, and the power to exercise control over others. Individuals have power in this twofold sense of potentiality for doing and of having power over other people, just as power in a social sense has this dual capacity to achieve in action and to impose a collective will. The dual nature of power is at the heart of much debate about its meaning and

41

implications, but for the purposes of this discussion what is most significant is the relation of authority to each facet of power.

Cicero's neat contrast between power and authority unfortunately becomes blurred once we examine the political reality behind his phrase. It is, for instance, arguable that the authority of the Roman Senate rested in part on its political importance as a governing, and not simply as an advisory body. Barrow observes that the constitutional struggles of the fourth century BC pointed by 287 BC to plebeian supremacy in the city. But the Punic Wars interrupted this process (*The Romans*, p. 50):

> two hundred years of war came, and the experience and wisdom and steadfastness necessary for the surmounting of times of strain and danger lay with the Senate. Its moral supremacy produced its supremacy in the whole conduct of affairs.

The Senate was a relatively small body able to ensure continuity of policy and rapidity in decisions, and included experienced administrators and soldiers.

Adcock confirms this view, noting that 'Rome's greatest enemy, Hannibal, unwittingly did her the service of making the authority of the Senate the necessary and natural expression of the continuing tradition of the Republic' (*Roman Political Ideas and Practice*, pp. 36–7). The Senate acquired the privilege of prolonging the term of office of consuls when necessary, the role of the arbitrator between generals with conflicting views, and control of the finances of war. Adcock comments that this increase in senatorial influence took place without any formal constitutional change, and without any conferring of *imperium* (command) or *potestas* (powers). What happened was 'a great increase of something the Senate already possessed – viz. authority, *auctoritas*, which was a mixture of prestige and initiative' (p. 39). Adcock also stresses the 'weight' which the collective opinion and advice of the Senate had, and the difficulty facing magistrates in disregarding the views emerging from senatorial debate, but adds that the Senate had not by law the right to veto the actions of the consuls or to prevent legislation by the plebs. Power lay strictly with the latter, but was not often exercised.

During the first century BC the continuation of wars and foreign conquests began to undermine the senatorial authority, since individual military commanders began to gain in prestige and became willing to use their troops to bid for supremacy in Rome. Despite Cicero's nostalgic backward glance to a republic sustained by the authority of its politically responsible aristocracy, stability returned to Rome when Augustus acquired unique authority as *princeps* of the Senate. While the Senate formally retained its old role and its old authority, it was in effect a shadow of its former self. Augustus himself claimed that as *princeps* he 'surpassed all men in auctoritas' (Adcock, p. 78). In practice, however, Augustus exercised not only supreme authority but pre-eminent power.

He preserved the forms of the constitution and the old offices of consul, proconsul in the provinces, and tribune of the plebs, but by jointly holding these offices he had the final word over each of his theoretically equal colleagues. His *auctoritas* therefore, unlike that of the Senate in republican Rome, was buttressed by specific legal power and by his command of the army. It was his successful exercise of power, in creating peace from civil war and maintaining Rome's world pre-eminence, that enhanced his personal authority, and won for him the title of Father of his Country. The authority which the Senate had lost was not recaptured when some later Emperors failed to conform to the semblance of constitutionalism. The Senate had lost its nerve, its previous prestige, and its previous political experience, and had been reduced to impotence.

It is worth noting one further evolution in the claim to *auctoritas*. During the fourth and fifth centuries AD the church of Rome inherited the legal and political ideas of the Empire and used them to clarify its own institutional and governmental status. It also inherited the Roman claim to comprise the civilized world and the Roman concern to ensure a continuity of tradition and inheritance, based in its case on the original act of foundation of the church by St Peter. Walter Ullmann in his account of these developments notes that the papal claim to superiority to the emperor, in matters touching the church, led Gelasius the First to contrast the pope's *auctoritas* with the mere *regia potestas* of the emperor. Ullmann's gloss (*A History of Political Thought in the Middle Ages*, p. 41) on these terms is:

> Both terms were in fact taken from the Roman constitution in which the 'authority' of the Ruler was over and above mere 'power': the 'authority' of the Ruler consisted of his outstanding qualification and was the faculty of shaping things creatively and in a binding manner. The 'power' referred to the execution of what 'authority' had laid down.

Arendt also quotes Gelasius in her discussion of the church's acceptance of Roman political ideas, but simply refers to the church claiming for herself 'the old authority of the Senate'. But, as indicated above, the idea of authority underwent a transformation when it devolved from the Senate to the *princeps* of the Empire. It is significant that Ullmann sees the claim to authority by pope or emperor as in effect a claim to sovereignty — and the relationship between authority and power suggested by his interpretation of Gelasius reduces power to the role of wholly subordinate executive, whereas in republican Rome the authority of the Senate could be overridden by the will of the people. As the church's interpretation of Roman political ideas laid the basis for the medieval legal and governmental tradition of autocracy, it seems reasonable to assume that the original republican concept of authority had been significantly altered since Cicero wrote.

If we try to isolate the original and essential meaning of the Roman *auctoritas*, it appears that in one sense authority did — as in Ullmann's interpretation of its later meaning — imply a superiority of wisdom and inspiration over mere execution of decisions. Arendt notes the greater admiration accorded to the 'author' than to the mere interpreter of his designs. The idea of authorship links up with that aspect of power which involves a capacity for action and achievement, and authority can be seen as initiator as well as guide in shaping policies. Authority in this sense is very closely related to the voluntary co-operation of people in order to achieve a particular goal, either in defining the goal, or inspiring people to act, or in giving weighty advice about the best mode of procedure. Authority which invokes voluntary compliance may even in a sense create and maintain that social power which derives from joint action. The usual semantic confusion between authority and power is partly explained by this intrinsic connexion. Moreover, the changing 'authority' of the Senate illustrated the fact that authority must continuously prove its potency, its effectiveness and its relevance to political life. On the other hand the Roman *auctoritas* originally existed independently of legally conferred powers and the ability to impose its will. The Senate therefore lacked the coercive power granted either by law or by the force of sheer numbers or by the ability to use force. Authority in its original sense is therefore to be distinguished from the form of power which flows from co-operative action, but is closely related to it. Rather than being contrasted with power *per se*, it can be most usefully contrasted with that form of power which involves imposition upon others, that is with coercion.

This discussion has so far concentrated on the Roman Senate because it is the prime example of political authority, but it may be more pertinent at this stage to translate these concepts into a more contemporary context. It is possible to explore the position of trade union leaders in Britain in terms of authority, co-operative social power and coercive power. Trade union leaders represent their unions both in the sense that they are elected to their posts by their members (the processes of election are not of primary importance here) and in the sense that they speak for the interests of their members in negotiations with employers and the government. So, in relation to their members and to the general public trade union leaders have authority; but they do not have the power to compel their members to follow their recommendations. Their role is to initiate policy, to advise their members to accept specific wage settlements, to clarify their own understanding of the best interests of the union. But if a rebellious minority defy union leaders there is in practice no way in which the leaders can impose their orders if their authority fails to carry sufficient weight. The final sanction of expulsion from the union is impracticable if many members are involved and is in any case almost unusable since it threatens to deprive the expelled member of his livelihood. Paradoxically, therefore, trade union leaders, often presented as the most powerful men in Britain, may find themselves impotent in relation to their own membership. This paradox derives from the fact that the 'power' of trade union leaders stems from the power created by the united action of union members. This power can be mobilized to carry through productivity deals; it can also be mobilized to bring an industry or a service to a standstill. In the latter case the power of numbers is being used coercively to bring to bear economic pressure on the employers. In a period when wage settlements are limited in principle by some form of incomes policy, strike power may also bring pressure to bear on the government to relax or abandon its policy. The government in its turn in this area of economic policy may be primarily reliant on the exercise of its authority, since any attempt to invoke measures of legal enforcement is, in the context of current British politics, liable to provoke the countervailing power of union action, which is capable of bringing down a government.

Authority and Coercion

There is a strong case for making an analytical distinction between authority and coercion, but it is still necessary to examine whether authority is in reality weakened by inability to use coercion when authority fails. If this is the case the practical and political significance of a distinction between authority and coercion is considerably reduced. There remain, of course, areas in which authority does exist quite independent of coercion – such as the area of professional knowledge. It is also possible to uphold the conceptual distinction while allowing that there may be a practical connexion between the maintenance of authority and the use of coercive power, as Peters briefly suggests. But the role of authority in politics is vitally affected by the question whether resort to coercion is a sign of the failure of authority, and therefore tends to weaken it, or whether coercion can sometimes strengthen authority. In the latter case we need to know in what circumstances coercion – which is taken here to mean all measures of law enforcement, but in particular use of physical force – might strengthen authority.

One answer might run along the following lines. It might be conceded that an institution which frequently resorts to force against dissident minorities has failed to exercise true authority over these groups. Nevertheless its ability to enforce obedience, or at least punish disobedience, strengthens its authority with the normally law abiding majority. Those individuals who might occasionally be tempted to disobey are discouraged by the threat of sanctions. In addition their general disposition to disobedience is encouraged by the knowledge that others breaking the law will be punished. Conversely, open disobedience, if not checked, might encourage further disobedience and so generally weaken respect for authority. So, limited use of force, which is socially sanctioned as justifiable, can indirectly strengthen authority by reinforcing the common disposition to automatic obedience.

The immediate point which can be made against this case is that it suggests why force is often necessary to *supplement* authority, which is the argument for government. It does not clearly show that force reinforces respect for authority, since reinforcing the disposition to obey is not the same thing. One reason why we tend to confuse the two is that we are socially conditioned by much of our experience to associate respect for authority with a fear of the consequences of disobedience. However, if we look at our experienced association of authority and force, we observe that the conditions which must obtain in order that use of force can strengthen a general willingness to obey narrows down very considerably the positive connexion between force and respect for authority. The force must be seen as legitimate in the sense that the body responsible has a right to use force; the reasons for using force must be seen to be fair; the degree of force must be seen to be proportionate to the offence and to general sentiments of what is tolerable; and force must be applied fairly to all offenders. If any of these conditions are not met the response is more likely to be indignation, rebelliousness or a loss of respect for the person or body concerned. These conditions for making the use of force compatible with the assertion of authority raise the question whether it is not the rules which minimize the negative effects of force, making it more congruent with the spirit of authority, rather than the force which strengthens the authority.

If we approach the question from a slightly different angle we can ask whether true willingness to obey can be influenced by the threat of force. If the threat of sanctions is the predominant reason for obedience, the obedience is likely to be withdrawn if one seems likely to get away with it. If the spectacle of other people flouting laws or rules with impunity encourages one to do the same, then it is clear that obedience to the law was not due to respect for the laws or the law giver, but at most to an awareness that everyone suffered from the same advantages and disadvantages in keeping to the law. There are conditions in which willingness to obey the law is dependent upon the behaviour of other people. If the basic purpose of a law will be destroyed by massive disobedience, then there may seem to be no point in the individual continuing to obey – if no one pays taxes then one's own contribution will not keep the health service going; and if obedience seems to entail personal risk then obedience cannot reasonably be expected – if most people illegally carry firearms, for example, it may be prudent to do the same. Hobbes rested his basic case for government on the proposition that people cannot be expected to obey the principles of morality at great personal risk or loss. Hobbes did however insist that one could be obligated in conscience to obey moral precepts even if this internal obligation was overridden by practical considerations. Similarly it is possible to distinguish between a desire to obey rightful authority and calculation, based on prudent self-interest, whether it is wise to do so if authority is not effectively recognized. The ability to enforce obedience may, up to a point, make willingness to obey authority square with self-interest (though there are definite limits to the effectiveness of pure force), but it cannot make people believe that obedience is inherently right.

There is however a more subtle case that respect for authority may be widely established in society, but any attempt to discard all forms of coercion overlooks the inevitable conflict between private interest and public good, and the internal conflict between the private person and the citizen. Authority represents the commonly recognized general good and the values of citizenship, but people need to have their social conscience reinforced by some form of coercion or sanction — for example when it comes to tax collection. Moreover people are aware that authority which is concerned with proclaiming and upholding social principles, like religious toleration or racial and sexual equality, has to maintain these principles against the convictions, prejudices and customary behaviour of sections of society, and may therefore have to enforce their observance. To adapt Rousseau, perhaps men must be forced freely to obey authority.

In answering this argument it is necessary to disentangle what is valid from those assumptions which are not. It is reasonable to deduce that in our capacity as sober and conscientious citizens we should accept a set of social rules and restrictions and entrust certain agencies with the responsibility of maintaining them, at times against our own inclinations. But this authority can only be totally effective if every member of that society gives free and voluntary consent both to the institution of authority and the rules it upholds. Since this total consent, whether given actively or tacitly, is impossible there is obviously a danger that in practice many people will not consent to specific laws and resent their enforcement, though this is not a serious problem unless a particular law arouses bitter opposition or unless people start to lose faith in the legislative authority itself. However, the fact that people do not freely accept all social rules means that we cannot strengthen authority as such by enforcing them against a person who refuses to accept that they are right. Embodying principles in the law is meant to put the weight of legal authority behind them so that people will come to accept them, but this kind of authoritative persuasion cannot be achieved directly by force.

If the argument that the need for widespread use of force against offenders indicates a weakness of authority is accepted, it follows that one possible answer to law breaking is not to urge even more punitive measures, but to consider whether a change in the law would promote more voluntary consent. Laws which are widely broken cannot be enforced, except haphazardly, and the effect of trying to oppose laws which a large section of the community does not accept is to drive the prescribed behaviour underground and to encourage other forms of criminal behaviour – arguments recognized in repealing prohibition in the United States. Wherever large numbers of people, normally law abiding, break a specific law it is a clear indication that the law is either unjust or at least that it fails to take account of social realities – arguments relevant to the debate about abortion laws. More complicated considerations arise when particular communities tend consistently to break the law – for example, the high crime rates in some slum areas. Although the nature of individual laws may be partially relevant, the central issue then becomes altering social conditions in such a way that the community ceases to be in a state of natural war with the wider society, and can therefore accept the justice and authority of the laws and institutions of the society. If this change requires fundamental alteration of class-dominated institutions or of racial attitudes, then society may continue to rely on forcible suppression of the poor or of ethnic minorities. On the other hand relatively democratic and egalitarian societies – in principle if not in social reality – are more likely to take measures to reduce perceived injustice and to seek to extend voluntary consent to the authority of law. There are times when upholding equality and justice may demand use of force, but where discrimination is upheld by a majority, or by a substantial minority, appeal to common authority and common principles is necessary before enforcement is possible.

So far it has been maintained that use of force cannot increase respect for genuine authority. There is however a psychological argument which somewhat confuses the distinctions drawn above: that is the respect we tend to give not only to what is right but to the person who is strong. This attitude can be understood and expressed in a number of ways at the level of personal relationships; when extended to the political arena its implications are different. Desire for a strong man is then often a desire for dictatorial power.

The readiness to respect a show of strength influences our attitudes when assessing the effectiveness of an authoritative body. A government may lose authority by seeming ineffective in carrying out its policies and failing to deal with problems facing the country. The *Guardian*, in a report on the confrontation between the Conservative government and the miners' leaders in 1974, quoted cabinet members as saying that 'surrender' to the miners 'would deprive the existing administration of any shred of authority to govern ...' (4 February 1974, p. 1). This example of the Conservative government failing to assert its authority over the striking miners reveals the ambiguity of the criterion of effectiveness, since the implication was that this effectiveness could be proved either by successfully winning over the miners, or having the power to compel their compliance with government policy. The concept of effectiveness is indispensable to political authority, which cannot in its nature be demonstrated solely by the objective value of its decisions unless people also comply with them. But it is perhaps necessary to refine the concept by understanding that what is at stake is effectiveness in gaining support and consent, and that it is a failure of authority to resort to force.

Our difficulty in accepting the idea that effective political or judicial authority might exist without having coercive powers reflects, as anarchists would be quick to point out, our conditioning within the political form of the modern state. Tribal societies studied by anthropologists provide us with examples of authority not backed by powers of enforcement — such as special mediators with ritual authority to end feuds, like the leopard skin chief who held such mediatory authority among the Nuer (Lucy Mair, *Primitive Government*, pp. 41–8). In so far as we have been thoroughly conditioned to associate effective authority with the ability to enforce commands our respect for bodies unable to do so will diminish. For example, the belief that the United Nations is impotent to maintain its proclaimed standards is probably one reason for loss of public respect for and belief in this international organization. On the other hand the more our political experience encourages us to believe that authority must be enforced, the less able we are to understand the nature of authority or to create new forms of it.

Authority and Bureaucratic Power

An analysis of government in terms of authority resting on consent on the one hand and of coercion — exercised through courts of law and ultimately through armed force — on the other, leaves out a large intermediate area of modern government. The increasing role of government provision and regulation, for example in directing the economy, in promoting welfare and education, and in controlling transport and town planning, involves the use of extensive powers and entails a large bureaucracy.

Administrative bodies enjoy in principle a delegated authority from representative government and are often referred to as 'the authorities', but they are not directly endowed with the right to issue orders by the public nor do members of an administrative bureaucracy individually have any claim to public respect. Their right to be obeyed stems neither from their representative status nor from a special expertise. It is true that some members of an administrative bureaucracy have been chosen for their professional or administrative skills, but an unskilled clerk of a department can issue instructions and expect to be obeyed. Administrative bodies are essentially anonymous. For this reason they are not directly accountable to the public for the way they exercise their powers: at most they are indirectly accountable through a representative assembly. Some countries introduce a greater degree of democratic accountability into administrative bureaucracy by extending the electoral system into the higher reaches of the government service and by refusing to safeguard the anonymity of public servants who justify their activities to elected representatives. For example, the administration is more anonymous and more indirectly accountable in Britain than in the United States. The ideal type of bureaucracy, as envisaged by Weber, does logically exclude election and guarantees anonymity for officials.

Administration cannot be viewed as an agency for coercion because of the nature of its political role. In the sense that government departments implement legislation or issue regulations or supervise other bodies, they do exercise powers of compulsion over the public in many areas of life, and can invoke sanctions for disobedience. However, the work of most government departments is designed to provide public services, or to regulate private behaviour for the public good, and therefore departments do in this sense act on behalf of the public and do enjoy a good deal of tacit consent and co-operation. They do not rely primarily on coercion.

Administrative bureaucracy can probably best be seen as an expression of the power of government, combining the co-operative power of rational organization, the specifically legal 'powers' granted by the process of legislation, and the social and economic coercive power of government ability to grant funds and give or withold permission to private bodies and individuals. There is of course room for considerable debate about the actual workings of government bureaucracy: whether the nature of bureaucratic organization maximizes administrative efficiency or promotes an inertia which makes government administration a power of obstruction to effective social action rather than a means of achieving it; whether administration is an instrument of a representative government or an independent power blocking various policies and legislation on the one hand and directing a wide range of activities without direct authorization from the elected representatives on the other; and whether most bureaucracies do pursue the public good or are in practice corrupt. But these problems are irrelevant to the fact that administration is the main instrument of government, and so long as the government itself is seen as legitimate the administration appears to serve the government; it is the main channel for the exercise of legitimate power.

Legitimacy

In practice there is inevitably a close connexion between our experience of political authority and our experience of government, and the connexion is particularly close in any régime claiming legitimacy. It is often difficult to find any very clear distinction between the normal use of the terms authority and legitimacy: the representative status of parliament, for example, appears to indicate both. The most obvious distinction to make is to attach the concept of legitimacy closely to the concept of government. In that case we might adapt Weldon and argue that 'force exercised or capable of being exercised with the general approval of those concerned is what is normally meant by legitimacy'. However, this definition is too narrow, since legitimate government implies use of a whole panoply of legal powers. Legitimacy like authority therefore implies recognition of a right to hold office and implies general consent to the rules of the political system, but whereas authority in its pure form is characterized by entirely voluntary compliance, legitimacy involves a right to enforce obedience, within certain agreed limits.

A second possible distinction between governmental authority and legitimacy is that authority depends both on acceding to political authority in the accepted manner and on exercising the authority of office in a way which is generally approved, whereas coming to power in the proper way seems more important in establishing legitimacy. During the lengthy debates about whether to impeach President Nixon, for example, it was never suggested that he was not at that stage legitimate President of the United States.

Legitimacy defined in terms of rules is a more static concept than authority. Although representative authority is closely linked to legitimacy, there is a distinction here between the form and the content of representation. The authority of an individual, a group or even an institution may wane while legitimacy is retained, since to deny legitimacy it is necessary to alter the generally accepted rules. In 1905, for instance, the Tsarist government could still claim to be the legitimate government of Russia, but for a time the St Petersburg Soviet wielded more authority, in the sense that its orders were widely obeyed and its actions effective. On the other hand a serious loss of authority threatens also a loss of legitimacy, since the government must rely increasingly on coercion, and revolt becomes more likely. Once an alternative locus of authority has been created it may eventually become an alternative government.

If legitimacy is defined in terms of established rules a government which has come to power by civil war, revolution or coup d'état cannot immediately claim legitimacy, although it may claim authority by virtue of its ideology, goals and popular support, by proving its effectiveness in meeting the country's needs, and by demonstrating the qualities of the new leaders. Weber's category of charisma is not really relevant to this form of personal authority, since it has overtones of hero-worship which are antagonistic to genuine authority. But charisma acquires a retrospective significance in the foundation of a new tradition of legitimate government, so that, for example, Stalin claimed for himself sole inheritance of Lenin's mantle.

Problems arise about the test of legitimacy – who has to recognize it? – and about differing levels of established legitimacy. If the test of a new régime's legitimacy is diplomatic recognition by other governments, then the normal practice is to recognize almost immediately any government which appears to have seized effective power. Diplomatic recognition confers a minimum and necessary status of legitimacy in relations between states and may assist internal acceptance of the new régime, but this minimal diplomatic form of legitimacy is compatible with a situation in which a government maintains its power through the fear, self-interest or apathy of a majority of its people. Promulgation of ideological justifications of the nature of a régime, new constitutions and legitimating rituals, like controlled referenda and elections, are part of the process whereby governments which have seized power try to establish new rules of legitimacy, and gain both international and internal recognition of them. The appearance of popular support may, however, be – and often is – a product of various forms of coercion. Time is a key constituent in creating legitimacy, in the sense that after say twenty years few people contested the legitimacy of Franco's government. But many of his subjects wanted a quite different régime in the future, as was demonstrated after Franco's death. The degree to which the legitimacy of a form of government is fully established is indicated by the extent to which individual governments may change without affecting the stability or rules of the régime, by the degree of genuine popular acceptance of it, and by popular assent to the kind of claims for legitimacy made by the régime.

If legitimacy is defined primarily in terms of the accepted political rules of a society, and secondly in terms of general acquiescence in the régime, it has both a *de jure* and a *de facto* element, but the two cannot be wholly divorced because *de facto* power tends to become *de jure*. In both aspects it is a morally relative concept. Both legitimacy and authority are in one sense relative to a particular context or set of rules, so one may recognize the legitimacy of a king without approving of monarchy, and recognize the authority of a political leader without supporting his party. But to identify authority does also imply some kind of absolute evaluation. One criterion for distinguishing legitimacy from authority is the role which force may play in creating and maintaining legitimacy. Provided the majority accept a government, legitimacy is not lost by use of force against a substantial number of citizens. Indeed a degree of governmental coercion may increase its stability and its claim to legitimacy based on the fact of obedience. Legitimacy may also be fostered and upheld by propaganda, that is by psychological forms of force and manipulation. Authority by contrast is characterized by an absence of coercion and requires voluntary and free acceptance, and thus to point to true authority does imply some kind of moral approval.

However, the most fundamental distinction between political authority and legitimacy is the one we started with: this is to see authority as an alternative to coercion whereas legitimacy is a justification for the use of coercion and therefore a concept rightly applied to governments. This basic distinction is also relevant when comparing authority and sovereignty.

Sovereignty

Authority and sovereignty are not always clearly differentiated in political language – indeed, as Ullmann indicates, there was in the Middle Ages a tendency to identify the two. But sovereignty is a much more limited concept, and the conditions for its existence are, even within popular usage, more precise. It is solely a political term and it also implies supreme and exclusive power. Its usage is closely associated with the development of autocratic styles of government. For example, the French legal theorist Beaumanoir, writing in the thirteenth century, styled the king 'souverain' over his barons, and allotted to him the right to decide personally what was, or was not, the law. The English use of the word sovereign to mean monarch indicates that sovereignty is especially associated with supreme individual power, but the concept has been generalized. But the belief that sovereignty must reside in one supreme will has caused continuing debate about the possibility of dividing sovereignty. Sovereignty also implies independence from other wills, and being above the law, as the term 'sovereign state' denotes.

The other main condition for the existence of sovereignty is an elaborate governmental structure – or state. Sovereignty was not a concept required by a small city state or by a truly feudal society. When power over a large territory becomes centralized, as in the Roman Empire or in the emerging European states, then the idea of supreme power becomes relevant. Sovereignty implies a hierarchy of power, or a bureaucracy, culminating in a supreme will.

Sovereignty therefore differs from authority in including powers of coercion as well as powers of initiation. It also differs from authority in suggesting the right to exercise a purely arbitrary will, whereas authority requires reasons. Sovereignty is indeed hostile to authority in the sense that sovereignty implies overruling all other wills and points of view, whereas authority implies an independence of executive power but a claim to be heard. Sovereign kingship was opposed to the independent authority of the law, of parliaments, and of the church. Whereas authorities in different spheres may co-exist, sovereignty tends to claim mastery in all spheres. The absolutist implications of sovereignty are explored to their logical limits by Hobbes, and can be extended from an individual to a popular concept of sovereignty.

Not only is the idea of sovereignty antagonistic to competing authorities, but it is also antagonistic to the authority which may have resided in the person or institution of the sovereign. The denial of any limits to sovereign power, or rules to guide the sovereign will, means that the right of the sovereign to command is grounded solely in the fact of supremacy – not in the wisdom of the sovereign's commands or his respect for the laws or his representation of the common good. These factors, if invoked at all, are not grounds for obedience, but secondary justifications for the exercise of supreme power. In reality the practice of sovereignty is tempered by custom and law, or by competing powers, and it may be limited by the continuing strength of authority within a particular tradition of government. Thus a 'pure' sovereignty is as rare as a 'pure' authority. But the idea of sovereignty is totally opposed to the idea of authority as embodied in the original Roman understanding of *auctoritas*. Sovereignty comes much closer, as some medieval writers indicated, to the rule exercised by a master or a *dominus* – that is to dominion.

Chapter 5
Authority in the Modern World

The previous chapters have examined the predominant models of authority handed down to us from the past and the attributes of authority in the abstract. It is now necessary to explore, however tentatively, the role of authority in relation to contemporary society. This chapter raises three main questions. The first centres on whether the problem of authority ought to be approached differently in the different spheres of life: whether conclusions about the need for authority in the home and school should be transferred to industry or politics or vice versa. The second issue is whether any form of authority is compatible with attempts to create a fully democratic and equal society, an issue raised provocatively by recent radical movements attacking the bases of not only political but also professional authority. The third question, which is discussed concurrently with the other two, is whether authority is necessary at all.

Authority in Different Spheres

Hannah Arendt raises in her work the general theoretical question whether there are intrinsic differences between various modes of experience and activity and whether or not it is appropriate to apply the same concepts and criteria to, for example, both child rearing and politics. This apparently abstract question is extremely relevant to immediate social concerns, such as the fear that a breakdown of authority in one area must affect society as a whole, since, if these spheres really are distinct, authority may only be necessary in certain spheres, and attitudes to authority may vary in each sphere.

Contemporary exponents of the need for authority are primarily concerned to prevent the extension of political democracy to the non-political spheres of the work place, university, school and home. This distrust of participation in decision-making from below, and of non-

55

authoritarian direction from above, reflects a fear that the demise of the old authoritarian model in these spheres will also mean the end of professional authority and of intellectual, moral and aesthetic standards. It also reflects the belief that the maintenance of authority, or its loss, is interconnected throughout society, so that authority in education is related to authority patterns in industry. G. H. Bantock, for example, in a critique of the over-enthusiastic application of progressive ideas to education, comments (*Freedom and Authority in Education*, p. 184):

> To understand the current uncertainty about the nature of authority in the schools it is, I think, necessary to see that such indecision only reflects the doubt and confusion that exist in wider social spheres.

He cites as an example quasi-democratic proposals like co-partnership in industry, where the 'old authoritative direction' is masked by democratic forms.

Given that there are different realms of life – the privacy of the family and the public realm of politics, work and education, thought and action – it is necessary to consider whether each sphere requires different types of authority or any authority at all. It is then necessary to examine the pressures toward unifying types of authority throughout a particular society.

For a clear awareness of the distinction between the private and the public spheres of life, it is helpful to turn first to classical Greece and then to the reassertion of classical ideas in the more complex society of modern Europe. The contrast between the household and the political arena was basic to Greek political thought. The Greeks distinguished between the persuasion among equals appropriate to the political sphere and the mastery of the head of the household over his wife, children and slaves, who were automatically excluded from politics. Work to maintain the necessities of life, which fell to the lot of slaves, also lay outside the public arena, and labour was therefore organized despotically.

The work of craftsmen, who were free men and had their own form of common assembly in the market place, was also distinct from politics. Arendt elaborates these distinctions in *The Human Condition* and finds the primary difference between craftsmanship and politics in the type of activity: the difference between making things, which is a solitary activity, and of doing and speaking, which must be in public. There is a parallel distinction between the world of thought, of solitary contemplation and of political action. Arendt argues that because the Greek concept of 'authority' drawn from the family was one of autocratic rule incompatible with freedom, and because politics itself lacked an authoritative element, Plato sought to transfer to the political realm images of authority derived from craftsmanship and, as his crucial model, from philosophy. Thus the philosopher élite in *The Republic* gained authority from its wisdom and ability to contemplate the Form of

Good. But because politics requires distinctive modes of activity, understanding and authority, the philosophic basis of élite authority could only be maintained by the 'noble lie', that is by political indoctrination. Arendt consistently claims, on the basis of the Greek distinction between different spheres, that different types of relationship are necessary, and that in the modern world the type of organization and activity appropriate to the political realm – participatory democracy – is not appropriate in any other sphere, and in particular that it is a mistake to try to realize it in the realm of work.

In modern Europe the distinction between spheres of activity was influenced by the medieval experience. One distinction which emerged was that between the sphere of religion and politics, as the modern state achieved independence from the authority of the church. At the same time trade was freed from the restraints of the church, a process hastened by the reformation, and to a large extent escaped the control of the state. The economic sphere not only developed independently of church and state, but freed itself from the previous links with the hierarchy of the extended family. The family became a more private and intimate sphere in which patriarchal attitudes still prevailed, but which began to include the notion of romantic love.

The previous Greek distinctions cannot be automatically applied to the newly defined spheres. The distinction between household and political realm in terms of the different types of rule appropriate to each was drawn less sharply at the beginning of the modern era because both inherited a patriarchal image of authoritarian rule, although distinctively political concepts of representation and the rule of law were also inherited from the feudal period. In contemporary terms the distinction is no longer valid because women have in principle been admitted as equals to the public realm and the household has become a sphere of equality between husband and wife. (The fact that this relationship is still influenced by law, custom and the church in favour of patriarchal attitudes is one of the issues pressed by the women's liberation movement.) The dimension of romantic love and of personal intimacy is also in principle incompatible with a concept of autocratic rule by one partner over the other, though love and sex can both be perverted into forms of domination. In addition the large and diversified household of the past did arguably require some form of rule and authority, but husband and wife do not need either to enable them to live together. Whereas the size of the household in contemporary Western society has decreased, and so eliminated the role of authority except between parents and children, the size of the state has greatly increased in comparison with the Greek city, thus enhancing the problems of rule, authority and stability.

In order to examine the kind of authority appropriate to the economic sphere, it is necessary to consider what has happened to the Greek categories of both craftsmanship and (slave) labour. It is relevant that the modern economic sphere arose out of the medieval economy of the guilds. It is also relevant to underline here the theory put forward by Kropotkin: that the medieval guilds provide us not only with examples of superb craftsmanship, but of impressive social organization. He comments on the sentiment of solidarity that prevailed in the guilds in which 'men of a craft were united, not only by the mercantile and technical sides of a trade but also by bonds of sociability and fraternity' (*The State*, p. 23). So Arendt's view of the solitary craftsman at work has to be supplemented by a view of the necessary co-operation between craftsmen in any major undertaking – building a cathedral for example – and of the co-operative organization which may arise from shared skill and interests. It is partly because the co-operative equality of masters within the guild was undermined by the new economy that work came to be seen entirely in terms of masters and hands. Though this relationship was in some circumstances softened by paternalism, with the development of industrialization it became increasingly impersonal and exploitative.

The designing of machinery and factory organization to achieve maximum division of labour reflected the autocracy exercised by early factory owners and the economic advantages of gearing the factory to absorb and train into an industrial routine cheap and unskilled labour, while skilled craftsmen became redundant. The result of industrialization was, as Marx with the classical Greek parallels explicitly in mind noted, to produce 'wage slavery'. Just as labour had meant the mindless and mechanical drudgery of slaves, so the division of labour in the factory meant the unthinking submission of the individual labourer to the co-ordination of the machine and the despotism of the factory foreman.

The development of trade unions represented the first stage in the workers' assertion of their economic right to earn more from their labour and their political right to organize to secure better wages and conditions of work. The trade unions mobilized the social power of the workers acting together against the economic power of the bosses. While the trade union movement has been closely associated with the democratic demand for the right to vote and the socialist demands for greater economic and social equality, and while trade unions in the West have achieved considerable economic and political power, trade unionism has remained primarily a defensive organization operating within the inegalitarian structure of capitalist society. As the more radical socialists have always argued, assertion of full political and economic rights by the workers and achievement of genuine equality requires transcendence of purely trade union consciousness and goals, and the claim to the right to exercise direct control over industry. This claim has always been espoused by more militant rank and file members and in moments of revolutionary fervour. Trade union leaders are now also prepared to espouse compromise schemes for worker participation on the boards of enterprises along the lines of the Bullock Report in

Britain or *Mitbestimmung* in West Germany; although it is arguable that such forms of participation or partnership by trade unionists are means of strengthening the mixed economies of the West and so totally opposed to socialist demands for worker ownership and control, they can also be seen as a necessary concession to the rights of labour.

In the post-industrial era the sophistication and flexibility of the machine is now available to eliminate previous drudgery. It also seems appropriate that the full recognition of the freedom and citizenship of labourers in the political sphere should have a counterpart in the conscious management of their own labour and its products in the industrial sphere. At the level of the factory as a whole this implies some form of elected workers' council with representative authority and the right to make decisions about the government of the enterprise. There are a number of inherent difficulties in making workers' councils effective – especially in a large and complex enterprise with a number of plants: for example, the problem of workers' representatives fully mastering financial complexities, the opportunities for managers to wield oligarchic powers despite formal democracy, and the question of how far the workers' council actually represents the interests of workers on the shop floor. But these are political difficulties which beset any attempt at representative democracy, not exclusive to industry.

On the shop floor itself it is possible to replace the authoritarian direction of management and foreman by the collective decision of the group, either by formal methods of direct democracy or by more informal arrangements. Some experiments in industrial democracy – for example the officially sponsored moves in this direction in Sweden – have included workers in certain factories taking over the organization of work in their section. Spontaneous initiative by British miners to end strict division of labour and to work the coal face in composite and self-regulating groups without external control or formal leadership, and a similar system of unsupervised gang organization of work in a Coventry tractor factory in the 1950s, are described by Colin Ward to show the greater efficiency and potential of flexible and informal modes of organization (see Krimerman and Perry (eds), *Patterns of Anarchy*, pp. 393–5). One advantage to this approach to industrial organization is that it introduces a greater degree of craftsmanship, or at least versatility, into the work routine itself and thus diminishes the element of mindless labour.

There would be two forms of authority in an enterprise organized on the principle of workers' control. A political authority would reside in the workers' council which, possibly in conjunction with representatives of consumers or of the local community, would also constitute the legitimate governing body of the enterprise. The other form of authority would exist whatever the formal organization of the firm: the authority of the specialist staff, the engineers, chemists, computer programmers. Within a work context the authority of the craftsman and the specialist is intrinsic to the work. But the 'authority' of a boss in the organization of a factory is the outcome of class relationships, hierarchical attitudes and conventional authoritarian assumptions about the nature of organization. Autocratic rule is no more necessary to economic than to political society. Indeed our modern ideal of political action stems as much from the medieval towns, the place where the free citizen and the master craftsman opposed the hierarchy of lord and serf, as from classical Greece; and the values of the 'burgher' (before he became the 'bourgeois' whose financial interests predominated over the responsibilities of citizenship) are closely associated with the ideal of disinterested craftsmanship.

The distinction between the political realm and the realm of education is, unlike those previously discussed, not one which can be erased or transformed by altering the structure, attitudes and technological level of society, because childhood is unalterably different from maturity. It is impossible to treat young children exactly like adults, and since childhood is a temporary stage everyone passes through, egalitarian arguments for self-rule do not apply. This does not of course imply that children have no rights, but that their rights are somewhat different from those of adults, for example the right to care and protection; nor does it necessarily mean that quite young children cannot benefit from a degree of self-government, a question discussed later in this chapter. It does mean that adult authority remains necessary.

Even benevolent adult authority over children may lead to a suppression of children's freedom. John Holt argues this case eloquently in his *Escape from Childhood*, in which he urges that children should be granted a whole range of adult rights, like the right to work, to travel and to vote. As Holt himself notes, this radical extension of children's freedom would not undermine the genuine authority of adults:

> We should note once more the distinction between natural authority, which rests on greater skill, knowledge and experience, courage, commitment or concern, and that authority which rests only on force, the power to threaten, punish, and hurt. Nothing that I propose here can lessen the natural authority of the parent over the child or the old over the young; indeed it will strengthen such natural authority as exists (p. 153).

Many of Holt's comments about the artificiality and adult manipulation of the institution of childhood are persuasive, but his argument for adult rights seems in general more relevant for adolescents than for younger children.

One problem now in deciding the proper role of authority in education arises from lack of clarity about when childhood ends. The progressive extension of the school leaving age means that those who quite recently would have been treated as near-adults, able to earn their own living, now come under the category of school children. It is not therefore surprising that the higher forms of secondary schools in particular should be inclined to demand adult rights of greater freedom and self-determination in ordering life at school.

Is Authority Interconnected?

Despite the theoretical case for a distinction between different realms, and between the types of authority appropriate to each, it is clear that there is a strong tendency to see authority in various spheres as interconnected. This view is rather like the domino theory held by American strategists faced with communist insurgency: if authority goes in the factories the schools will fall next. Its plausibility derives from the unifying tendency of the human mind. Faced with social complexity there are both psychological and intellectual constraints to see and react to a consistent pattern: to respect authority in all spheres or to decry it; to applaud equality or to fear it. Since this response is not confined to the theorist but applies to people in general, it is reasonable to assume that someone who begins to doubt or question authority in the state may be led to question it in the university, and conversely that recognition and respect for authority in, say, the home will reinforce it in the school.

Plato's picture of the decline in authority and order from the ideal state through forms of aristocratic rule to anarchistic democracy illustrates this view. He depicts the spirit of liberty entering into the home so that parents behave like children and vice 'versa: 'the father is afraid of his sons and they show no fear or respect for their parents'. In school 'the schoolmaster timidly flatters his pupils, and the pupils make light of their masters'. In society in general the old fear to be thought tyrants by the young, men and women and slaves mix on an equal footing, and rulers are forced to grant the people unlimited freedom (*The Republic*, pp. 282–3).

When specific movements are attacking one form of authority, the contagion of ideas and the tendency to emulation (especially under the influence of the mass media) do make it likely that at least limited rebellions will spread from one sphere to another. Student protests against the state turn inwards against the universities. School children take up the slogans and methods of university students, and both appeal to the ideas and methods of militant trade unionism. Women's liberation movements have followed on political dissent and taken up some of the arguments of black power. These movements are primarily directed at the abuse of power, exploitation or discrimination, but they naturally involve attacks on forms of existing authority in most spheres of society.

Nevertheless it is equally clear that attitudes to authority in one sphere are not necessarily and always reproduced in another. There has been a considerable time lag between the introduction of political democracy in the West and contemporary, tentative, attempts to extend the principles of democracy to economic and pre-political spheres. Even the modification of authoritarian attitudes within the family, school or firm has been gradual and by no means consistent throughout a particular society. One reason appears to be that it is possible to maintain political ideas about equality and government by consent at a level of abstraction which does not necessarily impinge upon the realities of everyday life. For example, the egalitarian ideas implicit in Locke's contract theory could be held within an authoritarian and patriarchal society. This kind of incongruity can be accepted without much strain partly because the nature of political theorizing encourages generalization and rhetorical commitment, which may be confined to the realm of books and speeches, and partly because the existing society and social attitudes prescribe which social groups count as political persons. Thus the Athenians automatically excluded foreigners and slaves from their polity, some Levellers excluded servants from the category of men, and many nineteenth-century democrats excluded women from the category of people. It can also be accepted because the family, school, work place and politics are in fact usually seen in everyday life as largely separate realms, in which different rules of behaviour apply and different relationships are appropriate. So despite pressures towards a unified view of authority, the realms are also to some extent insulated from each other.

However, all social spheres are subject to long-term changes under the impact of industrialization and its associated social and political trends. It is therefore reasonable to expect that aristocratic types of society will have authoritarian types of authority in all spheres, and that democratic types of society will have comparatively non-authoritarian types of authority. At this stage it is necessary to consider whether a wholly democratic and egalitarian form of society is compatible with any kind of authority at all.

The relationship between democratic and egalitarian values and the maintenance of authority can be usefully explored in a context which is the subject of much topical debate and soul-searching – education. It is illuminating to contrast Hannah Arendt's views on this issue with some progressive experiments in non-authoritarian education.

Authority and Education

The issue of authority in education is complicated by the dual role of the teacher: as representative of the social and moral standards and requirements of the outside world, and as specialist in a particular branch of knowledge. It is possible to argue either for authoritarian discipline or for democratic methods in the first context, while stressing the need for a different approach to teaching itself; but in practice the two roles are more difficult to separate. The tendency of schools to use authoritarian and punitive measures, both in maintaining good behaviour and in actual teaching, led educational reformers to argue for radical changes in both aspects of education. The spread of permissiveness in educational theory has prompted the reaction that educators have abandoned necessary authority and discipline in both areas – a position taken by Arendt in her essay on education (*Between Past and Future*).

She sees the disappearance of authority within American schools as part of a wider crisis in education, which she attributes to progressive ideology. The first assumption she identifies is that children should as far as possible be left to govern their own world, and that therefore 'the authority that tells the individual child what to do and what not to do rests with the child group itself' (p. 181). She argues that as a result the adult loses contact with the child and becomes helpless in relation to him. Second, the individual child is no longer subject to the authority of the adult (against whom he can rebel), but the tyranny of his peers. The child cannot rebel against this tyranny, cannot reason with it, and cannot escape from it. So he must either conform or take refuge in juvenile delinquency. Arendt is transferring to the level of the school the political distinction between an authoritarian society, which is hierarchical but leaves a degree of freedom, and tyranny, which reduces all citizens to an equality of powerlessness. However, it is not the individual tyrant she seems to have in mind, but the more insidious tyranny of the group. The implications are grave not only for the child but for the wider society, because adults no longer introduce children to the reality of the outside world and an understanding of its traditions and values. It is only when they have been educated into the world that they can as adult citizens take responsibility for changing as well as conserving their society. What Arendt means by authority in education is not entirely clear, but she appears to have in mind an adult certainty about social standards and an ability to transmit them to the children in their care.

It is interesting to compare Arendt's comments on American education with those of Erich Fromm in his forward to A. S. Neill's book *Summerhill*. Fromm argues that adult control is still exercised in the class-room in American schools, but it is an anonymous rather than an overt form of adult regulation. The sanction for disobedience is 'not corporal punishment but the suffering face of the parent, or what is worse, conveying the feeling of not being "adjusted", of not acting as the crowd acts' (p. x). Teachers have therefore debased progressive education by confusing non-authoritarian education with hidden coercion, and have to some extent hidden their authority behind that of the child's peer group.

In order to clarify whether authority can be separated from authoritarianism in education, and whether it is compatible with real self-government by children, it is helpful to look at a genuine experiment in progressive education, of which Neill's Summerhill is a good example. Summerhill deliberately granted the children self-government through a democratic General School Meeting, which allowed the children to discuss and vote on the regulation (or non-regulation) of all aspects of social life, including punishments for breaking the rules. This democratic form of government does not bear any resemblance to Arendt's picture of the tyranny of a majority of children over their helpless peers for a number of reasons. The first is that the authority of the school meeting was not anonymous: its rules were based on clear reasons and could be amended by majority vote. The procedural rules of democracy provide some guarantee of individual rights in comparison with the undefined rule of group opinion, which is probably created by certain dominant personalities. A further guarantee was provided at Summerhill by the fact that children of all ages took part in the General Meeting and as elected officials. Neill comments:

> Good self-government in a school is possible only when there is a
> sprinkling of older pupils who like a quiet life and fight the
> indifference or opposition of the gangster age. ... Children up to, say,
> twelve, on the other hand will not run good self-government on their
> own, because they have not reached the social age (p. 52).

So those on the threshold of adulthood therefore educated the younger children into social awareness and behaviour. Third, the adults in the school shared the responsibility for the government of the school, by taking part in the discussion and making proposals. Although adult votes had no more weight than those of the children, and Neill insists that he was often overridden, the staff's presence meant that they could not stand aside from responsibility and that the children had to listen to them.

Outside of the school meeting adults at Summerhill did exercise various forms of power and authority directly. Neill describes how he would, if necessary, step in to control an individual child, for example when he found a little boy threatening to hit other children with a hammer. He distinguishes here between 'punishment' for disobedience of adult authority, and 'learning that one cannot go about hurting others for one's own gratification' (p. 67). Neill had unchallenged authority as psychological guide and describes how if a case of stealing arose, the pupils would consult him about whether to bring it up at the meeting or leave the case to Neill himself. He also had final power in certain areas, such as to hire and if necessary fire staff, and to send away as a last resort a child who could not be integrated into the community. Although Neill is anxious to minimize the role of adult authority in life at Summerhill, its role in creating a community and setting a 'tone' which make self-government workable appears to have been of considerable importance. Despite Summerhill's indifference to many conventional rules of behaviour, there were clear limits set to allowable freedom, based on mutual respect between pupils and staff for individual rights, including rights to privacy and property. Neill himself draws a theoretical distinction between freedom and licence. These standards of social conduct were ensured and transmitted by the staff and older pupils, but especially by Neill's own presence and personal authority. Summerhill can therefore be seen as an experiment in education which combined democratic self-government with adult authority, but where the role of authority was largely confined to maintaining conditions favourable to good self-government and dealing with difficult and disturbed individuals.

Another progressive experiment in non-coercive education has tried to maximize rather than minimize adult authority, but authority understood in a highly specialized sense. The Cotswold Community approved school differed from Summerhill in taking only maladjusted and delinquent children, and this fact may have influenced the nature of the experiment which occurred. David Wills traces the evolution of the Community from a strictly hierarchical and punitive discipline to a much freer and more informal rule under a new head. He characterizes the first régime as one in which 'all authority, all responsibility, was vested in one man, the headmaster, who was at the top of a chain of command, so that the staff were in a sense prevented from exercising authority in their own person' (*Spare the Child*, p. 24). Discipline was enforced by regimentation, shouting and punishments, including corporal punishment inflicted by the head. Parallel with this formal hierarchy was an unofficial hierarchy created in the underworld of the boys, based on the tyranny and brutality of a few senior boys, and on an elaborate system of protection. The new head sought to destroy both the formal authoritarian hierarchy and the informal system of tyranny. The new régime included allowing the delinquent boys to work off some of their repressed hate and frustration by smashing up the place. The abolition of the old system of controls, and the opposition of many staff members to the change, resulted initially in a semi-breakdown of discipline. The reorganization of the school focused on offering the boys, especially some of the most deprived, the affection and personal care they had never experienced. But the head's main attempt was to create a new form of authority, partly by delegating responsibility for different aspects of the school's work, partly by encouraging each staff member to be a source of independent authority. Wills describes the ideal as follows:

> They had to be men, moreover, of authority who knew and were able to show that authority is not something that depends upon a system of controls handed down through an hierarchy, but something within a man; something that arises from his own integrity and confidence in himself, and which makes those around him feel safe (p. 24).

It has been argued earlier that authority is not strictly 'something within a man', but with this caveat Wills's analysis is illuminating. The authority of the staff had a dual function. One was to create a model of adult masculinity to replace the previous model of sadistic dominance created by the boys' sub-culture. It is relevant here that Arendt, when discussing the Roman concept of authority, notes that 'the auctoritas maiorum became identical with authoritative models for actual behaviour, with the moral political standard as such' (*Between Past and Future*, p. 123). In Wills's definition authority is personified not in the past, but in the immediate experience of the boys. The second function of the staff's authority was to control the boys by indicating clearly the limits of acceptable behaviour without resorting to force or rigid institutional rules, or on the other hand becoming indiscriminately permissive.

The much greater emphasis on adult authority at the Cotswold Community than at Summerhill can be seen as a response to the emotional backwardness of the boys, who required not only the affection, but also the security of authoritative control they had lacked as young children. It is also arguable that the conflicts involved in overthrowing the old hierarchy and system of values among staff and boys were not conducive to making democratic government on the Summerhill model immediately viable. But there is also a theoretical difference of approach – Neill emphasizes freedom and equality between children and adults in most respects, while Wills in his interpretation stresses the gap between children and adults and adult responsibility for transmitting standards of social behaviour. The idea of authority which Wills promotes, urging the responsibility of those in authority to stand for a set of values and to uphold them, but at the same time underlining the difference between coercion and authority proper, seems to be reasonably close to Arendt's understanding of authority.

Authority of a different kind is at issue in the actual teaching in progressive or other schools. Arendt complains that the American system of training teachers tends to minimize the importance of the subject matter, so that the teacher does not know his or her own subject. As a result (*Between Past and Future*, p. 182):

> the most legitimate source of the teacher's authority as the person who ... still knows more and can do more than oneself is no longer effective. Thus the non-authoritarian teacher, who would like to abstain from all methods of compulsion because he is able to rely on his own authority, can no longer exist.

What is at stake here is a tradition of academic education and the values attached to that tradition. Bantock comments that 'unless the respect for authority, the authority of the subject, the authority of the teacher (which derives from the subject) exists, learning becomes impossible' (*Freedom and Authority in Education*, p. 189). The importance of a tradition of learning is not for Bantock simply a matter of scholarship, but of the existence of objective and transcending cultural values which inform the life of the individual and society.

This approach underlines the dependence of the authority of any professional on a respected tradition. This link between authority and tradition – a link elaborated upon by Carl Friedrich in *Tradition and Authority* – explains why the erosion of accepted traditions leads to what is perceived as a 'crisis of authority' not only in education but in other professions.

Professional Authority and Libertarianism

Doubts as to whether any form of authority can exist in a society receptive to theories demanding radical application of democratic and egalitarian ideas to social organization have been posed most sharply by the various libertarian movements which arose in the late 1960s and which extended their political discontents to other spheres of social life. Precisely because they have pursued the apparent logic of direct democracy and commitment to equality to extremes their views are relevant to an attempt to clarify in principle the role of authority.

In particular libertarian movements have questioned the validity of professional authority. Radical newspapers experiment with collective editorial decision-making and dispense with a formal editor; radical theatre companies do without a director and give the players equal say. Group therapy is urged to replace the relationship between omnipotent individual psychoanalyst and his patient. Women's liberation groups urge women to take more responsibility for the care and control of their own bodies instead of relying on the paternalistic authority of doctors. University students demanding democratic control over the organization of the university often claim the right to determine what they are to learn and how it should be taught. Even organizations which are less radical see it as natural to claim democratic rights not only in ordering social life but in professional spheres. For example, the officially recognized Union of Secondary School Students in Sweden, to which about one-third of secondary schools belong, espouses not only democratic rule in the classroom but the pupils' right to have a say in drawing up the curriculum, which considerably reduces the authority of the teacher as the person who knows what must be learnt and in what order.

All these examples illustrate the tendency to assume forms of authority are interconnected, and that if it is undesirable in one sphere it is necessarily undesirable in another. But it would be misleading to see commitment to direct democracy or anarchy as the sole or even primary cause of hostility to authority in the professional sphere. Equally important is the fact that the libertarian, like the conservative, equates authority with authoritarian rule, and that the revolt against patriarchalism is seen necessarily as a revolt against all authority. In so far as professional authorities do tend to claim omniscience and demand absolute obedience and acceptance of their superior knowledge, the confusion between authority and authoritarianism arises from immediate experience and personal resentment.

The radical critique of the authority of psychologists, doctors, town planners or teachers is often prompted less by opposition to authoritarianism than by opposition to the presuppositions and practices of these professions. It can be argued that various forms of therapy and medicine rely too much on drugs and too little on awareness of the personal needs and problems of the patient, or that patients are subordinated to the rules of bureaucratic and hierarchical institutions, or that psychological theory and therapy in various forms are geared to making individuals conform and adjust to inherently unjust and exploitative societies, or that resources are misapplied to prestige technology like heart transplants instead of simpler measures which would benefit far more people. Architects and town planners may be accused of putting arid criteria of design above adapting buildings to a human scale, planning for cars before people, or ignoring the needs of the community in the interests of efficiency. Academic disciplines are under attack in the university for the irrelevance of the aristocratic tradition of classical education, the way in which social sciences especially reflect the ideology of capitalist society, and the degree to which universities have abandoned an independent, critical and humane stance in order to service this society. Education in schools may be attacked on similar grounds, and also on the grounds that it attempts to process working-class children into middle-class culture while denigrating their own authentic culture, or to brainwash black children into accepting white imperialist values and despising their own heritage. It may be criticized even more fundamentally as inculcating irrelevant knowledge and skills to the detriment of more vital forms of education acquired in the past by children brought up in the countryside or apprenticed to some practical skill.

Since authority is closely related to traditions, the eroding of a tradition of education, for instance, will naturally undermine the authority of the teacher. But it is very important whether this is seen and decried as a further instance of the demise of all authority in society, or rather as evidence that a tradition of education needs renewing. The first view leads to attempts to reimpose authoritarian discipline in education and other spheres. The second view involves looking more closely at the confused strands and ideologies which comprise 'traditions' of education and most other professional disciplines and clarifying what is valid and relevant and what is not.

It is also important to be clear that democratic and libertarian views are not opposed to all forms of professional authority. There are a wide range of crafts and skills which are essential to society, and in these spheres it is extremely improbable that even the most consistent anarchist would contest the authority of an expert. Authority becomes contentious when it is linked to a rigid hierarchy — such as when a senior journalist acquires the powers of an editor and uses them autocratically, or a senior architect claims the right to mastermind all the designs in his office. The anarchist or democratic alternative here is for more flexible organization and communal responsibility, which is in principle quite compatible with the essentially non-hierarchical nature of professional authority. Professional authority becomes much more contentious when it entails power over laymen, either directly over people or through political decisions which affect the whole community, and is open to much more serious abuse. Obvious abuses are checked to some extent by the ethical code and rules of a profession, but the more subtle claims to omniscience and dictatorial power are not. It is, however, fair to argue that it is in the interests of a truly disinterested professionalism to consult the needs and wishes of those concerned as far as possible. The doctor who gives authoritative advice but leaves the patient free (where possible) to choose, or the town planner who consults people in the locality about his plans, is not only adopting a democratic rather than an authoritarian approach, he is being more genuinely professional. In relation to political bodies the role of the professional is normally advisory, but his advice cannot easily be set aside. The potential for abuse of authority here lies in the likelihood that some experts will permanently have the ear of government and they may well give partial advice excluding contrary professional opinion.

The libertarian solutions for these problems are to break down authoritarian attitudes and modes of running institutions, whether mental hospitals or planning departments, and to promote decentralization of political power, thus breaking down the monopoly of particular experts. Citizen participation in running hospitals or parents on school governing bodies may also be a means of checking professional authoritarianism. A more radical break with past paternalism or manipulative attitudes can however only occur from within professions. At this point what is required is the evolution of new schools of thought backed by successful experiments and authoritative exponents of new approaches; for example, R. D. Laing is often cited in critiques of orthodox psychiatry. The tendency of libertarians to rely on their own preferred professional authorities is evident from their writings and noted by their critics – such as Carl Friedrich – and is not in fact self-contradictory (given the necessity of some form of authority in professional spheres) provided their trust is not the uncritical adulation radicals sometimes accord their heroes.

To conclude this discussion of authority and democracy: commitment to direct democracy or anarchy in the socio-political sphere is incompatible with political authority, but this approach is not necessarily or wholly destructive of all forms of professional authority. But democratic attitudes do tend to encompass some professional spheres, partly because of a confusion between coercive rule and professional authority, and partly because political assumptions are applied to areas where they are strictly irrelevant. For example, it is reasonable to argue in egalitarian and democratic terms that a director or manager should not have sole and autocratic rights to hire and fire actors, decide which plays are to be staged and the casting for them. But it is ridiculous to argue that it is 'undemocratic' for an actor to accept the overall interpretation and advice of a director. If in the spheres of craftsmanship and learning authoritarian concepts of hierarchy are out of place, an egalitarianism which denies degrees of skill and experience and the role of the professional division of labour is just as irrelevant. It is truer to see the relationship between the actor and director, or the instrumentalist and the conductor, as one of 'mutual authority' than of subordination and command. If there is a case for, say, informal and collective direction of plays, it is the quite different anarchist argument for unstructured organization: that the end result is better because everyone's talents are fully and enthusiastically used.

Is Authority Necessary?

The discussion so far has suggested that there is one sphere in which authority is irrelevant – between two or several people living together as lovers or friends. There are three spheres in which some form of authority is necessary and intrinsic: the relationship between adult and child, teacher and student, and professional and layman. Authority in these spheres may be abused or insufficiently authoritative, but unless it exists child rearing, education and professionalism are impossible. And there are two spheres in which the role of authority and the claims of democratic egalitarianism are highly debatable, but which may be approached from the same theoretical standpoint: the organization of a work community and of a social community. It is the value of political authority which requires further consideration.

The case for some forms of collective and direct decision-making at the level of relatively small groups – on the shop floor, in a housing collective, or at street or parish level – is persuasive; and, assuming a fair degree of common interest and shared belief, there is no need for authority. The larger the political unit and the more diverse the interests and beliefs incorporated within it the greater the need for some type of political authority. The value of representative as opposed to delegate assemblies increases in principle in complex societies because a delegate necessarily reflects a relatively narrow and coherent constituency; if he does not he cannot be clearly mandated as a delegate, and a representative assembly at a national level is therefore more capable of balancing interests and standing above purely sectional viewpoints and commitments to seek a general good.

This argument for representation is based on the logic of delegation and representation respectively and assumes that in both cases delegates and representatives act upon ideal principles. The reality of course is different. Self-seeking, the drive to power, corruption and blatant disregard for the interests either of electors or the society as a whole are quite often the norm in politics. It is this fact which helps explain the appeal of professional models for politics and the desire to extinguish politics in favour of authoritative direction by specialists. By comparison with the profession of politics most other professions retain an image of shining integrity. It is also the bad reputation of professional politicians in many circumstances that gives negative impetus to the devices of direct democracy – restriction on the number of times political office can be held, recall and referenda. Indeed the devices associated with the ideas of direct democracy and delegation may have been invoked as often in an attempt to ensure that a representative fulfils his role faithfully as to replace representative democracy by delegation. This would be at least partly true of the populist movement in the United States around the turn of the century and of the anti-corruption movement in India in the mid-1970s.

However, it is the very danger of corruption or of power-seeking that makes it more urgent to establish forms of political authority which will command respect. Wherever there is centralized executive power it is important to balance it by an independent representative authority. Constitutional authority is also necessary at state level in order to lay down agreed rules of political behaviour and ensure some degree of continuity and stability. The role of a constitutional court, if it achieves genuine authority, is also potentially a significant check on arbitrary executive power.

The strongest argument for upholding some form of authority in the political sphere is that it is one guarantor of the moral and social standards of the community. As the influence of customary modes of behaviour and of religious faith decline, the importance of authority to reinforce and reformulate standards increases; and where an old society has been deliberately overthrown political authority is directly responsible for fashioning new values and standards of behaviour. Despite the fact that conflicts of power and ideology are most intense in the political realm, it is within a political framework that the problem of adapting forms of authority to contemporary conditions has been most successfully resolved: through the evolution of legal tradition, through constitutionalism and representation. The possibility of a stable authority is clearly related to historical and social conditions, but it is also possible to create and foster political action and to escape from the determinism of social and cultural inheritance.

Chapter 6
Authority and Revolution

The problem of authority in revolution arises at several stages: in seizing power; in maintaining it; and in transforming social relations and standards when it is necessary to replace the old authority patterns and beliefs. The importance of authority in a revolutionary context is often overlooked because it is usual to think of revolution primarily in terms of violence, and of revolutionary government in terms of force. This is not simply an image projected by those afraid of revolution – though it has been elaborated by conservative theorists and by historical myth. It is held at least as strongly by many theorists and protagonists of revolution – including those who in practice have paid due attention to the political and psychological as well as the military aspects of revolutionary success. Mao Tse-tung for example is misleadingly associated with the philosophy that 'power grows out of the barrel of a gun'.

The tradition of political thought has also contributed to the association between images of violence and the act of creating a new and fairer society; Plato in *The Republic* uses the image of the artist who scrapes his canvas clean before proceeding to design the city of his imagination. But there is also a body of political reflection on the close and necessary association between the founding of a new state and the exercise of authority. The authority of the laws accepted by the states of classical Greece often stemmed from an original great law-giver, from a Solon of Athens or a Lycurgus of Sparta, who vested his creation with his personal authority. Rousseau, in discussing the figure and inspiration of a law-giver in the foundation of a state, provides at the same time a definition of the kind of authority required (*The Social Contract*, p.87):

> as the lawgiver can ... employ neither force nor argument, he must
> have recourse to an authority of another order, one which can
> compel without violence and persuade without convincing. It is this
> which has obliged the founders of nations throughout history to

72

appeal to divine intervention and to attribute their own wisdom to the Gods; for then the people ... obey freely.

Hannah Arendt argues that an essential element in the Roman *auctoritas* was the sense in which it embodied the values of those ancestors who had engaged in the sacred act of founding the city, and that the only recent act of foundation which has generated a political authority able to ensure political stability was that of the American founding fathers who did create a new state out of revolution.

Since revolutions are necessarily associated with violence, it is helpful to start by clarifying what role violence does play before considering the problems of creating authority. Military force may certainly be crucial to ensure the victory of a revolutionary party. Although both the February and October Revolutions in Russia were achieved with scarcely any fighting, the Bolshevik government had to defeat the White Russian and foreign armies before the revolution was secure. In China the communists came to power as a result of winning a civil war and the Yugoslav revolution was won in the course of a national liberation war against occupying forces and consolidated by use of force against political opponents at the end of the war. The act of revolution is however quite distinct from civil war, since revolution depends upon mass popular support, commitment to a new order and on spontaneous initiatives to create a new society. Revolution itself may be bloodless.

There are two other forms of violence closely associated with the experience of revolution. The first is mob violence. A distinction must be made between the capture of power at the centre, which may result from the disintegration of the old régime, and the overthrow of the authoritarian institutions and old ruling groups in society as a whole, especially in the countryside. The latter may result in outbursts of uncontrolled popular violence by those previously oppressed. Peasant uprisings against their former landlords are frequently violent – the more brutality used by landlords in the past to exact rents and services, the more likely that retribution will be bloody. Jack Belden records in *China Shakes the World* the beating and execution of hated landlords by enraged Chinese peasants, who swept aside the idealistic communist students who tried to stop them. The upheavals in Chinese social relationships also released the fury of women who had been forced to submit to brutality and humiliation by their husbands. Women's Associations would descend in groups on recalicitrant husbands, beating them viciously and forcing them to bow down to their wives. This spontaneous popular violence against hated members of the old society is a probable if not inevitable result of a revolution. It is interesting that in recent revolutions this popular vengeance is most likely to be reserved for the secret police, true of the generally self-disciplined crowds in both Budapest in 1956 and in Lisbon in 1974.

The other form of violence most often linked with revolution is organized terror, symbolized first by the tumbrils rolling through the streets of Paris. The necessity of terror in order to defend the revolution, a belief eloquently propounded by Robespierre, was accepted by the makers of the Russian Revolution, who would refer back to the great bourgeois revolution in France to justify Bolshevik terror in the socialist revolution, although in the honeymoon days immediately after forming a new government they hoped to avoid such measures (see, for example, Carr, *The Bolshevik Revolution 1917–23*, pp. 153–6). What is meant by terror needs clarification. Three characteristics of revolutionary terror suggest themselves: a tendency to indiscriminate suppression – Dzerzhinsky said the Cheka must conquer the enemy 'even if its sword falls occasionally on the heads of the innocent' (Carr, p. 167); its use against whole classes of people who are treated as automatically suspect; and its use against all political groupings who maintain any form of opposition to the ruling party, even if they have also backed the general aims and principles of the revolution.

Since violence is opposed to authority and potentially destructive of it the important question which arises is to discover which forms of violence during a period of revolution are compatible with the establishment of a stable authority later, and which are not. Civil war does not necessarily destroy the possibility of a future revolutionary government based on mass popular support; nor does that spontaneous violence which erupts against members of the former dominant class while the old order is being overthrown. Both forms of violence can be seen as intrinsic to the actual victory of the revolutionary party, and both are finite in time. There is a much greater likelihood that officially sponsored terror will be used in lieu of authority and will erode authority, whether it is used during civil war, against the supposed continuing danger of counter-revolution, or to promote a further stage in revolutionary class struggle – for instance against rich peasants. Relevant factors influencing the likelihood and extent of terror are whether the civil war occurs before or after the revolutionary party has come to power; whether or not one party has established its right to represent the social classes behind the revolution; and how this party interprets its role once it has come to power. The significance of these three factors can be observed by comparing the Russian, Chinese and Yugoslav revolutions. In both the latter the Communist Party successfully established its claim to be the party of revolution, and in both it came to power after a war of national liberation that enabled the communists to assert their role as defenders of national unity and independence. In both cases the communists were able to strengthen and extend their authority by political measures in the course of the war.

Winning Authority

The Chinese communists achieved ultimate victory because of their success in identifying themselves with the cause of Chinese nationalism, winning the support of the peasants and embodying aspirations for fundamental social change, and because their opponents were politically discredited by 1949. They gained prestige and recruits during the 1930s by their call for resistance to Japanese aggression and by their guerrilla campaign against the enemy forces during the war with Japan, when they achieved a popular reputation as the most committed fighters for China's national independence. Parallel to their patriotic agitation and action the communists undertook consistent programmes of radical social reform in the areas under their control. Even in partisan areas behind the Japanese lines they took over the land of absentee landlords, reduced land rents, introduced primary education and drastically altered the status of women. These changes were carried out under a united front government in which Communist Party membership was limited in order to include all on the spot prepared to unite against the Japanese, and to encourage political activity among the poor peasants who could choose their own leaders.

In the subsequent civil war between the communists and the Kuomintang it was the communist sponsorship of the redistribution of land, of an end to landlordism and of the creation of a new village democracy which won the support of the Chinese peasants. The Red Army also observed extremely strict discipline in relations between soldiers and peasants, and so ensured that the Army should be seen as friend and protector of the peasants, not as oppressor. Jack Belden notes that during the war between Mao's forces and Chiang Kai-shek from 1946 to 1949, he saw peasants travelling miles to give pigs and chickens to the communist soldiers. Belden's account underlines the degree to which the communists in this period had won the respect and confidence of the peasants (*China Shakes the World*, pp. 615–6):

> Peasants often told me: 'The Eighth Route Army is just like your own father and mother'. The Communist Party put it the other way around: 'We are the descendants of the people; the people are our ancestors.' Nothing could illustrate the nature of Communist power more clearly than this. When you look on another force as your own father and mother, you are recognising that force as the only authority in life. And you are going to fashion all your hopes, actions and ideas on the moral codes set up by this force which claims to represent the general will.

The Yugoslav communists also claimed to be the only group of true patriots, prepared to fight for the liberation of their country from occupation by the fascist powers. This claim was strengthened by the fact that the Yugoslav government had surrendered ignominiously when the country was invaded and its leaders had fled into exile. A group of royalist officers had raised guerrilla bands (the Chetniks) to continue resistance and were backed by the émigré government in London, but they soon abandoned direct attacks on the Germans, which provoked terrible reprisals, and later there was clear evidence of their collaboration with the occupying forces. The communist-led Partisans on the other hand adopted an offensive strategy against the occupying powers.

The Yugoslav communists' authority as representatives of Yugoslav nationalism depended however not only on their guerrilla campaign, but also on their political policy in relation to the complex nationalities question inside the country. The Yugoslavia that was created in 1919 comprised six territories which were diverse in culture and religion and already divided by nationalist conflicts and ambitions. Mutual rivalry between Serbs and Croats, the two dominant nationalities, had bedevilled inter-war Yugoslav politics, with Croat extremists threatening secession from the Serb-dominated Yugoslav kingdom. The Axis powers capitalized on these antagonisms and carved Yugoslavia up into a number of quisling territories. The fascist government of the new Croat 'state' greatly intensified existing fears and hatreds by sponsoring the systematic massacre of the Serbs living in their territory. The Chetnik forces led by Serb army officers were animated by a crude Serbian nationalism and so took sides in the fratricidal struggle. The Communist Party and the Partisan army on the other hand condemned these excesses and put forward a consistent policy, implemented except for a few local lapses, of promoting the brotherhood and unity of all the Yugoslav peoples. All the nationalities within Yugoslavia were incorporated into the Partisan forces. This stand endowed the communists with both moral and political credit and made them the only representatives of a truly Yugoslav patriotism. They reinforced this immediate call for unity by projecting a political future in which Yugoslavia would become a federal state in which no one nation would impose upon the rest.

Like the Chinese Communists, the Yugoslav Party based their claim to become the legitimate government on a programme of radical social change. During the Partisan struggle People's Committees were set up in villages and regions of liberated territory and these Committees were proclaimed the basis of a new people's government which would rule after the war. Two formal Congresses of the Anti-Fascist People's Councils at the end of 1942 and 1943 symbolized the extent of this new political organization and asserted their authority as the genuine representatives of the Yugoslav peasants and workers in place of the royalist émigré government.

The Yugoslav communists were by the end of the war in a favourable political as well as military position. They were able to prosecute a civil war against the royalist Chetniks in the course of a final drive to liberate their country; they had both the power and authority of a legitimate government to prevent a return of the old régime, whose representatives were in exile; and in settling their accounts with their enemies they could appeal to the popular hatred of those who had collaborated with the occupying forces. If the Yugoslav communists' road to power can be called a revolution, it was a revolution directed from above, drawing on the national and socialist aspirations of the Yugoslav peoples, but never dependent on spontaneous movements from below. It was a complete contrast with the situation faced by the Bolshevik Party after February 1917, acting in a context where the impetus for the revolution had come from the people, where a number of left-wing parties were competing for their allegiance, and where despite the fall of Tsarism the Provincial Government still represented predominantly the middle class and liberally inclined aristocracy. The Bolsheviks had to consider whether they could and whether they should seek to seize power and promote a second revolution, and the issues of both power and authority were of decisive importance.

The Russian Revolution

A dual form of authority and government existed in Russia between February and October 1917. The Provisional Government, despite the later access of some moderate socialists to the coalition and changes in leadership, never enjoyed real support among the workers, soldiers and peasants, who looked instead to the Soviets which had sprung up in the cities and the countryside. Within the dualistic framework the Soviets enjoyed greater authority by virtue not only of their popular base but of their representative status as elected bodies. The Soviets also wielded more effective power in the running of everyday life, since they controlled the factories, the means of communication and the army more directly than the government. In the absence of a constituent assembly the Soviets were the only elective bodies, and since they were subject to frequent re-election they were also an index of changes in the popular mood.

The status of the Soviets was of peculiar interest in the development of a form of revolutionary authority. This style of organization, based primarily on the factories, had sprung up spontaneously during the revolution of 1905. Trotsky wrote of the Petersburg Soviet of that year (*1905*. p.122):

It was an organization which was authoritative and yet had no traditions; which could immediately involve a scattered mass of hundreds of thousands of people while having virtually no organizational machinery; which united the revolutionary currents within the proletariat; which was capable of initiative and spontaneous self-control.

He also recognized that the Soviets' authority depended on their breadth of representation. The experience of 1905, and in particular the prestige then enjoyed by the Petersburg Soviet, set a precedent for 1917, so that the authority of the 1917 Soviets rested on an embryonic revolutionary tradition, which was to be reinforced by the events of that year.

The Bolsheviks, who launched the slogan 'All Power to the Soviets', could appeal to both their democratic and their class character in comparison with the Provisional Government. But the Bolsheviks also had to accept that initially they were in a minority in the Soviets, where both Mensheviks and Social Revolutionaries enjoyed much greater support, so their immediate role was a persuasive one. When the All-Russian Congress of Soviets met in Petrograd in June only a sixth of the delegates were Bolsheviks, but a mass demonstration in the capital showed strong support for Bolshevik slogans. The different pace of revolutionary momentum in the main cities and the provinces created a dilemma for the Bolsheviks, who felt constrained to hold back so long as they lacked significant support in the provinces, but as a result were losing their hold over the militant workers, soldiers and sailors of Petrograd. The latter fear led them to associate themselves with the abortive armed demonstration of the July days, as a result of which they were temporarily discredited.

The Bolsheviks regained the initiative, and their authority among the workers, by leading the defence of the Provisional Government against the supposed coup by General Kornilov. Immediately afterwards the Bolsheviks gained a majority in elections to both the Moscow and Petrograd Soviets. Lenin called on the Mensheviks and Social Revolutionaries to seize power and rule through the Soviets and promised that the Bolsheviks would act as a legal opposition; when they ignored this appeal he felt vindicated in his belief that the Bolsheviks alone represented the true revolutionary interests of the Russian people.

When in September Lenin began to press his Party to plan for a takeover of power, the issues of power and authority were both raised sharply. Whereas Lenin believed that the mood of the people and of the army would favour a bold and immediate seizure of governmental power by the Bolsheviks, some members of the Central Committee feared that the Provisional Government could call on sufficient forces to make such an attempt abortive and disastrous. A different disagreement arose between Lenin and Trotsky. The former was concerned with the military aspects of overthrowing the Provisional Government, and anxious to act rapidly to pre-empt further attempts at counter-revolution. He therefore proposed the Bolsheviks should undertake the action in their own name and on their own authority. Trotsky was in agreement that the balance of forces could be tipped in favour of overthrowing the government, but concerned to ensure the political legitimacy of a seizure of power by clothing it in the authority of the Soviets. The Second All-Russian Congress of Soviets due to meet in the capital in October promised an opportunity. Since the authority of the Soviets stood much higher among the people than that of the Party, and since commitment to Soviet democracy was very strong within the ranks of the Bolsheviks themselves, he was seeking to safeguard the authority of the future Bolshevik government.

As President of the Petrograd Soviet at this stage, Trotsky was well placed to implement his own strategy, and he was aided by rumours early in October that the government meant to leave Petrograd for Moscow and so abandon the centre of the revolution to the Germans. The Petrograd Soviet used this as an excuse to take over the defence of the city, and its Military Committee thus acquired legitimate control over the surrounding troops, while other socialist parties could not protest against actions on behalf of the Soviet. Trotsky then directed public attention to the need to safeguard the holding of the Second Congress of Soviets. The seizure of power was thus carried through under the guise of a purely defensive action on behalf of Soviet legality. Dietrich Geyer comments (Pipes (ed.), *Revolutionary Russia: A Symposium*, p. 225):

> Success was assured by the steady increase of the authority of the Petrograd Soviet. ... Even some members of the Military-Revolutionary Committee may have believed that they worked exclusively to defend the garrison against counter-revolutionary pogroms.

The Second Congress met as the transfer of power was being completed, and the Bolshevik delegates (in a majority at the Congress if their Left Social Revolutionary supporters are included) gave the stamp of legitimacy to the takeover of power and elected a Bolshevik government.

The new government's authority remained fragile, however, since the other socialist parties in the Congress of Soviets denounced the Bolsheviks' actions, and there was strong pressure from some unions, for example the Railway Workers, for a coalition socialist government. Some Bolsheviks supported this proposal, fearing the immediate dangers if the Bolsheviks were isolated and the long-term implication that a purely Bolshevik government would have to rely on terror. Another serious challenge to the authority and stability of the new government was posed by the results of the elections to the Constituent Assembly that met in January 1918. The Bolshevik deputies numbered only one-quarter of the total in the Assembly, and the majority of the seats were held by their opponents, the Right Social Revolutionaries, who had most support among the peasants. Rather than tolerate this authoritative challenge to their government, the Bolsheviks disbanded the Assembly. This move did not totally discredit the revolutionary legitimacy of a party which based its right to rule on its ability to represent the vanguard of the proletariat, and not on a parliamentary majority, and which could still fall back on its support in the Soviets. But the Bolsheviks' alienation from the other socialist parties with mass support among the peasants and workers, and their inability to keep the support of the numerically much smaller but militant anarchist groups, meant that from the outset they had to rely on force as well as authority in upholding their rule, even among their natural supporters. By 1921, after the crushing of the

Kronstadt rebellion, the Bolsheviks had lost their claim to legitimacy based on the Soviets, since they refused to hold new elections to the Soviets; and they had lost their authority among the social groups which had once supported the Party.

Maintaining Revolutionary Authority

During the process of seizing power the authority enjoyed by a revolutionary party is necessarily uncertain in its extent. Once in power the party must endow itself with a more enduring authority to consolidate the gains of the revolution and to carry through a transformation of society. One factor of some interest in this connexion is the type of governmental tradition inherited by the revolutionary régime. The Bolsheviks came to power in a country accustomed to Tsarist autocracy, and although they set out to repudiate this heritage they came to reproduce Tsarist measures of coercion in more savage form. By contrast the Chinese communists could draw on a concept of government, which, despite its profoundly authoritarian nature, was based on the precepts of Confucianism, which urged rule through the 'power of virtue' and moral suasion. The ideal of government naturally differed from the reality, and in the century preceding the communist victory the dissolution of empire and the warlord era had meant frequent rule by pure violence at all levels. But the Chinese communists could combine their aim of restoring unity and independence to China with the restoration of a new unifying authority. C. P. Fitzgerald commented in 1958 that observers had been surprised how much the new régime relied on words rather than violence, and noted that: 'It was a very old and strong conviction among all Chinese that the use of force is an admission of failure; a doctrine central to Confucian teaching' (*Flood Tide in China*. p. 51). In basing this new authority on Marxist doctrine, but Marxism already given a distinctively Chinese form, the communists could combine a tradition of respect for doctrine with a message relevant to the needs of the peasants and workers of contemporary China. The Chinese Party has therefore tended to rely heavily on exhortations from above, has encouraged debate and criticism – though within strict limits – and emphasized 're-education' of opponents. Fitzgerald cites a former prominent Kuomintang general who had been given an important post. There is no doubt that the moral suasion practised by the Chinese is both socially and psychologically coercive, especially when directed against opponents, but most commentators agree that it has enabled the régime to avoid the mass executions and imprisonments which characterized the Soviet régime, though the extent of direct violence used against opponents immediately after the Civil War and later is subject to dispute.

The chief source of authority, however, must be the revolution itself, whatever the heritage of political ideas and practices from the previous régime, and all the devices of symbolism, ceremonial and myth-making are usually invoked to celebrate this act of foundation. The name of the state is changed and so are its flag and anthem; the forms and nomenclature of the offices of state are changed and styles of official ceremonial and public dress transformed; the names of cities and streets are altered to honour the founders of the new state and expunge reminders of the old régime; old memorials are often pulled down and new ones raised; public festivals are given a new political meaning; private dress and manners reflect the new spirit of equality. The French Revolutionaries began a new calendar, and though no later revolution has declared quite such unbounded optimism, the sense of a new beginning has inspired those taking part in the building of a new state. Over the years the myth of revolution may well be elaborated in song, dance and drama, repeated in public performance and taught to children in the schools, as in Cuba and China. The revolutionary foundation can often be linked to a longer tradition, either of a national movement or of the world socialist movement, so that the Paris Commune and the October Revolution reinforce the symbolic significance of later communist foundations.

The creation of revolutionary myth is up to a point a natural process, which has positive value so long as it reflects a genuine popular feeling and response, and does not result in serious distortion of historical truth and current political reality. When one party invokes the myth to invest itself with permanent and exclusive power then the myth is turned into Plato's 'noble lie', and easily becomes a justification for the abuse of power.

One central problem for the party of the revolution is how far it can or should claim a special authority to safeguard the goals of the revolution, even against the popular will. This potential conflict between an ideal general will and the immediate expressed majority will is inherent in any form of government, and the idea of representation – as already noted – involves some commitment to uphold what is seen as the real interest against immediately perceived interests. This conflict between an objectively understood general good, as interpreted by the government, and the requirements of democracy is more acute where a revolution has been attained through considerable suffering and where the risks of counter-revolution are still real. The justifications for the dictatorship of a vanguard party in the name of the dictatorship of the proletariat also appear strong in the circumstances of civil war, famine and economic chaos. The Bolshevik Party faced these dilemmas in 1921, when it decisively rejected the possibility of compromising with the other socialist parties or surrendering power to them, and therefore also rejected the right of the people to democratic representation through newly elected Soviets, since they knew that a disillusioned and weary people would probably leave the Bolsheviks in a minority in the Congress of Soviets which selected a new government. Although the Bolsheviks had managed to lead their countrymen to military victory in the war with the White Russian armies and foreign interventionist powers, they did so at the cost of losing mass support and their resulting political actions constituted a moral defeat.

When it abandoned its claim to legitimacy embodied in Soviet democracy the Bolshevik government also lost much of its authority and had to rely instead on increasing coercion and violence. The Cheka silenced socialist and anarchist critics. The Party became responsible for the bloody suppression of the Kronstadt rebels who were demanding a return to Soviet democracy. The trade unions, who now had the greatest claim to represent the workers, were also subordinated to the Party. Parallel to the forcible elimination of opposition and criticism among the people as a whole, the Party leaders drastically curtailed the previous freedom of debate and of democratic participation enjoyed within the Party. The absence of reasoned criticism outside and inside the Party encouraged autocratic modes of operation and the assumption of party infallibility. The less genuine authority the Party enjoyed through proved effectiveness in tackling economic disaster and in eliciting voluntary co-operation, the more it had to fall back on force and regimentation – or in the case of the peasants on the temporary expedient of reintroducing economic incentives as an alternative to forced requisitions.

How far the Bolsheviks' actions in the early 1920s were made necessary by the desperate circumstances of the early post-revolutionary years, and how far the trend towards rule by force might have been reversible under different leadership in later years, are both questions open to debate. They lie however outside the scope of this chapter, as does an analysis of the Stalinist era. What is much more relevant to the theme of authority is to examine the experience of a party which set out to reject the Stalinist heritage, and to achieve socialism under the guidance of a party which avowedly relied more on its influence than its coercive powers. The ideas and actual practice of the Yugoslav Party since it was expelled from the Cominform in 1948 are extremely suggestive about the problem of a party which seeks to rule through authority alone.

Authority and the Yugoslav Party

Soon after the break with Moscow, the Yugoslav leaders began to criticize the excessive centralism and bureaucracy which had, they believed, deformed the Russian state and Party. To avoid these dangers in their own country they introduced formal workers' control in the factories (1950) and devolved much greater powers to the unit of local government, the commune, in 1952. Both these innovations were heralded with theoretical manifestos, but the initial practical steps were largely symbolic. By the mid-1960s however the central government had delegated substantial powers, including control over investment, to individual enterprises, and the communes also enjoyed considerable autonomy. The framework of workers' control (self-management in Yugoslav terminology) had been extended from the factories to all places of work and to the schools and universities. Direct public participation in social and political life was also promoted through housing communities and through voters' meetings. These forms of participation and direct democracy in the sphere of government and the economy were designed to make possible the gradual withering away of the state. They also threw into relief the importance of the role to be assigned to the Party within this framework.

The Yugoslav leadership did envisage parallel changes in the role and organization of the Party, which were publicized at its sixth congress in 1952. Tito told the delegates that the Party would cease to occupy a privileged position in society. Party policy should not in future be implemented by issuing orders to factories and local government bodies; instead Party members must influence opinion by arguing for the correct policies. Party members would earn respect by their hard work and integrity and political understanding, and would not fall back on coercion. This move away from a leading role to a persuasive and guiding role in society was symbolized by changing the Party's name to the League of Communists.

It is questionable how far a real as opposed to rhetorical change in the Party's role was envisaged, but it is worth underlining the theoretical implications of the new idealized role. In the distant future the Yugoslav theoreticians looked to the withering away of the Party as well as the state; the ultimate aim was a partyless democracy of multiple elected councils and a large measure of direct democracy at a local level. Consistent with this ideal of 'Soviet' democracy the Yugoslav constitution-makers have tended to favour rotation of offices and limitation on the re-election of representatives in local and federal assemblies in order to avoid creating a permanent class of professional politicians. But despite an elaborate institutional framework of self-management untrammelled democracy is reserved for a future when the Yugoslav people have attained a fully socialist consciousness. In part this means that the communists are not prepared to allow democratic wishes to overthrow the socialist system they fought to create. It also indicates a realistic understanding of the prerequisites of total democracy: a high degree of common interest, common values and a common ideology. In the Yugoslav context the conflicts of interest and attitude to be overcome arise not only from class but from national differences. Thus it is the Party's role to transcend these differences and avoid the possibly reactionary results of total democracy.

The role of the Party, as envisaged in the official theory, was to act as an authority. The Party embodied the revolutionary aspirations and socialist idealism which had inspired the founding of the new state in 1945, and was therefore both symbol and guarantor of these values. The Party's political task was to demonstrate these values in the practical example of its members, and to help create the social conditions which would make socialism a reality. This dual role of exemplar and guide could however be fulfilled only if on the one hand the Party enjoyed popular trust and support, and on the other the quality of individual communists reinforced this readiness to listen to the Party's advice. It was also of course necessary that Party policy should prove to be effective and so reinforce the weight of the Party's proposals.

The Yugoslav Party's ability to become a contemporary and revolutionary version of the Roman Senate, guiding policy through its authoritative advice but leaving final power with the people, has been restricted by a number of factors. The Party leaders never contemplated giving up their grip on central government within the foreseeable future. This was scarcely surprising, but it added to the difficulties of the Party's role at local levels, since this unwillingness to abandon central power extended, for example, to a refusal to allow dissident candidates to stand for chambers of the republican and federal assemblies and made the Party control nomination of candidates. Even where the central leadership urged local members to rely on authority rather than coercion, the latter were often very ill-suited to the sophisticated part they were asked to play. The local Party bosses in the early days were mostly Partisan veterans badly educated if not illiterate, accustomed since 1945 to throwing their weight around, and often corrupt.

Other problems have arisen because of the limits to the active support which the Party could command. For example, peasant involvement in the Party was lost after the attempt at collectivization, initially supported by the peasants, proved a failure and was abandoned. The new student generation, bored with the Partisan myth, have tended to stand aside from the Party, either ignoring politics or finding inspiration in New Left or national beliefs. The workers have been largely alienated because workers' control has proved unreal, and because the economic policy of market socialism has resulted in great inequalities of income and not cured problems of inflation and unemployment. Most serious of all, the nationalist rivalries which the Party hoped it had overcome, and which were largely suppressed in the 1950s, reasserted themselves in the liberal climate of the late 1960s, immobilized the federal government, split the Party itself and threatened secession by Croatia in 1971. Reacting against the divisive ambitions of renewed nationalism Tito has tried to recreate a monolithic and disciplined party, wielding frankly coercive powers, to act as a unifying force. During the late 1960s it sometimes appeared that Tito himself was the only symbol of united Yugoslavia and the only authority holding the country and Party together.

The Yugoslav Party's perhaps temporary abandonment of its attempt to turn the Party into an authority divorced from direct power can be ascribed largely to the special difficulties facing a party in an underdeveloped and nationally divided country. But it was also inherent in their conception of the Party's role that it should meet considerable difficulties in any society. It requires, for instance, a very nice judgment to act and speak authoritatively in such a way as to carry weight without imposing decisions. Yugoslav communists who did stop giving direct orders tended to sit back and let democracy take its course. The Party's symbolic and moral role as guardian of socialist principles is also hard to combine with its involvement in daily politics and administration. Whereas the Supreme Court in the United States, for example, stands aside from direct political pressures, the Party cannot. The multiplicity of its functions and role in government also means that the Party must act as a supposedly objective arbiter in areas where it is inescapably partisan – such as in deciding how much overt and organized dissent to allow. Whatever authority resides in the Party is therefore constantly in danger of being converted into a legitimation for exclusive power and its abuse. This danger is reduced if the Party is prepared to bind itself by deferring to other forms of authority, like that of representative assemblies and the judiciary. (The Yugoslav Party moved in this direction during the 1960s and set up a Constitutional Court as well as allowing a fair degree of parliamentary independence.) It is also reduced by freedom of debate in the press and within the Party, which requires reasoned exercise of authority. But no measures can eliminate the inherent disadvantages of vesting authority in an organization like a political party designed for the capture and exercise of power, especially in view of the historical connotations of the Communist Party's role ever since the Bolsheviks set the pattern in the early 1920s.

Charismatic Authority

One question raised by all three communist revolutions that have been discussed is the significance of the individual leaders who have been treated as personifications of the revolution. Do Lenin, Mao and Tito qualify as examples of charismatic authority? The answer partly turns on problems of definition, and it was argued in chapter two that authority in its pure sense is incompatible with the kind of magical dominance denoted by the term charisma, though the connotations of this concept coined by Weber are in any case far from precise. The evidence we have about Lenin, Mao and Tito in the period prior to their coming to power reinforces this distinction between authority and charisma. Each of them had personal authority due to exceptional ability and strength of personality, but none of them commanded a godlike supremacy over their immediate associates or over the people who came in contact with them. For example, after the February Revolution Lenin won over a doubting party to accept his militant strategy and later he imposed his aim of insurrection on a hesitant Central Committee, but his authority did not prevent some of his closest associates defying him both before and immediately after the takeover of power. Indeed if one is looking for a charismatic figure during the course of the events of 1917,

Trotsky with his oratorical brilliance is a more likely candidate, though even he could not always sway the Petrograd crowds. Mao Tse-tung and Tito emerge, like Lenin, as energetic and admired leaders, but as leaders dependent upon the very capable and intelligent men they had gathered around them.

After the takeover of power the need to establish the legitimacy of the new régime became predominant, and in all three cases the leader of the Party has been built up in the public eye as a heroic figure whose virtues and foresight are a testimonial to the wisdom and revolutionary virtue of the government. In Lenin's case the personality cult was established after his death and its purpose was to demonstrate the legitimacy of his heirs. Because Lenin died soon after he had founded the new state his legacy is double-edged. On the one hand his body lies in the Red Square mausoleum sanctioning the socialist claims of the rulers in the Kremlin; on the other, his last will and testament to the movement, expressing his doubts about the future, gives powerful support to those who wish to claim the heritage of the October Revolution but denounce the distortions since Lenin's death.

Both Mao and Tito lived long enough to impress the stamp of their own personalities upon the course of their new states. Their role became a dual one: in one sense each remained simply *primus inter pares*, a political leader surrounded by powerful colleagues and potential rivals; yet each has been projected as the symbolic founding father of the revolution and as one above normal criticism. The public persona then strengthens individual influence. Certainly Tito, although the honour paid to him was not comparable to the homage paid to Chairman Mao, achieved unrivalled personal influence which is a combination of his personal authority and political competence and of his symbolic importance within the state. Whether the fact that Tito and Mao continued to preside over their régimes for so long promoted stability is debatable. It clearly avoided the distractions of a power struggle in the early years, yet the more Tito has been identified as the sole guarantor of Yugoslav unity and stability, the more awareness of a succession crisis has contributed to potential instability. In China Mao's role, for example in promoting the Cultural Revolution, was not stabilizing in the normal sense, though he could have been seen as a guarantor of the continued purity of the revolution. Events since Mao's death do not suggest his real influence has outlived him.

There is an interesting anomaly in the fact that régimes founded on revolution, which demands above all the action and initiative of a broad mass of people, should seek legitimacy through exaggerating the charismatic qualities of an individual founder. It is possible to speculate about a universal tendency to associate an act of foundation with a superhuman personality and to appeal for evidence to classical Greece and Rome. But the habit of mind which imagined mythical origins, believed that the dividing line between divinity and humanity was often bridged and practised civic religions, is clearly alien to contemporary rationalism, and it would be rashly ahistorical to assume some common psychological impulse. The Greek figure of the legislator is more compatible with modern beliefs, but is clearly inappropriate as a model for the revolutionary, who does not propose settled laws but radical and ongoing change. It is also arguable that even if a modern tendency to look for godlike leaders or to revere dead heroes does exist (or that political uses can be made of former religious impulses), a revolution which sets out to transform social relations should overcome superstitious, adulatory and submissive attitudes. The tendency to elevate a party as the sole instrument of revolutionary ideals and to elevate one man as the representative of the revolution can be seen as both a moral and political betrayal of the original principles of the revolution.

Revolution Without Authority?

It is appropriate at this stage to raise a fundamental problem which the discussion has so far bypassed. If the idea of revolution essentially depends upon a popular upsurge of feeling and is marked by the degree of spontaneous and creative activity by large numbers of people, why is there any need of authority at all? Perhaps all attempts to create a revolutionary authority are necessarily examples of false authority and a guise for usurping the power and potential created by popular action.

In order to approach a satisfactory understanding of this issue it is necessary to distinguish between the phases of revolution. The first phase may take the form of a mass uprising or insurrection, and may be wholly spontaneous and lacking any previous organization or political leadership, except at a very local and *ad hoc* level. Both the 1905 and February 1917 Revolutions in Russia were insurrections in this sense, whereas October 1917 was not. Insurrection represents an anarchist ideal since it displays in pure form the power and the initiative of the masses and the irrelevance of either political parties or individual leaders, whereas guerrilla warfare or any planned attempt to seize power requires structured and hierarchical organization.

In the second phase, after the old order has been overthrown, some form of organization must emerge to maintain economic and social life. The economic organization which emerges most naturally in the factories is a worker's council to take over control of production. The response of the peasants depends on their basic aspirations and social consciousness: in Russia they took over the land of former landowners and divided it into private plots; in Spain the peasants of Catalonia and to a lesser extent of Andalusia (who were under anarchist influence) collectivized the expropriated estates, and in some cases their own private plots as well. The political form which sprang out of the experiences of 1905 and 1917 was the elected Soviets, a model of revolutionary political organization which can be traced back to the Paris Commune and its districts in the 1790s and forward to Hungary in 1956.

One question which arises from the distinction drawn between delegated and representative assemblies in chapter five is how far these popular councils have been expressions of the spirit of direct democracy antagonistic to older concepts of representation. Both their organization and electoral procedures have reflected an uncompromising belief in democracy, since as Marx claimed for the 1870 Paris Commune the council is conceived as a working as well as a legislative body, its members receive no special privileges, and both individual delegates and the council as a whole are directly accountable to the electors and subject to frequent re-election, which means that councillors must reflect the immediate and changing moods of the people. Nevertheless the councils or Soviets have inescapably acquired an aura of authority, because they have represented the aspirations of the artisans or workers against the dominant classes and their institutions. Thus both in 1905 and 1917 the Soviets claimed revolutionary authority in contrast with the existing government. Second, a Soviet at the level of a city like Petersburg necessarily tended to acquire a good deal of independent initiative and wide-ranging responsibilities which made it a source of authority in the eyes of its electors and people from outside the city. So although the Soviet was much more directly responsive to the popular mood than any parliamentary assembly, it formulated plans and took action with the confidence of a representative body and led the people of the capital with authority. Moreover the Congress of Soviets meeting at several removes from its original electors naturally tended to be seen primarily as a representative and symbolic body, not just as a delegate assembly. Indeed the strict application of delegation, like direct democracy itself, is impracticable outside a very narrow and small circumference.

From a purist anarchist standpoint, therefore, even the Soviet system of self-government is open to criticism, and Kropotkin did in fact argue that the 1870 Commune was an irrelevance and that spontaneous initiative was more effective and creative in resolving specific problems like housing the homeless, and feeding the city dwellers. But it is difficult to assess the long-term effectiveness and authority of a truly Soviet system of government because the Soviets' strength has depended on short term revolutionary élan and not been tested over a longer period of normality. Moreover even in these revolutionary conditions their activity has been affected by the role of various political parties or groupings within them. Political parties which by their nature tend to be centralized in organization, to hold relatively uniform policies and to manoeuvre for dominant power within elective assemblies, are in contradiction to the decentralized nature of Soviets and to the concept of delegates directly acting on the wishes of their electors on specific issues.

If in practice both Soviets and political parties are likely to wield a degree of independent power and to claim the authority to direct policy and to pursue revolutionary goals, the modified case made by many anarchists, for example in the early years of the Bolshevik régime, that revolutionary governments should rely on popular initiative rather than stifling it, remains immediately relevant. The dangers of an élitism which relies on a revolutionary vanguard and fails to meet the needs or enlist the support of the majority of people – in the case of Russia, the peasants – have also been effectively stated in anarchist writings. The inability of the Bolsheviks to gain voluntary peasant co-operation in increasing food supplies and in delivering them to local towns was a sign of the ineffectiveness of the régime in this crucial respect, and as suggested earlier a failure of authority. Popular initiative and political authority are not incompatible so long as both are working in the same direction, and responsive to one another. On the contrary their combination can be seen as necessary to a free, creative and responsive society – the alternative is regimentation, bureaucracy and governmental force. Authority is therefore necessary not only to ensure stability for a revolutionary government, it is necessary to maintain the spirit of innovation and initiative often associated with revolution and to avoid the tragedy of revolutionary violence institutionalized as terror.

Social Transformation

It is inherent in the meaning and nature of revolution that there should be a transformation not only of the forms and nature of government, but of social and personal relationships throughout society and thus of social values. During the first phase of a struggle to overthrow the old régime a revolutionary movement will derive much of its support and its fervour from those sections of the population with most to win from the overthrow of old forms of oppression. In the case of workers and peasants this is so obvious as to be a truism, though the much greater significance accorded to the peasants in the Chinese, and even the Yugoslav, revolution is of interest from the standpoint of Marxist theory. What is more unexpected is the force for local change unleashed in China by mobilizing the women in favour of a new social order. The domination of men over women had been intrinsic to the structure of the Chinese family and indirectly to the authoritarian hierarchy of Chinese society founded on the family, and was presented in Confucian philosophy as part of the natural order of the universe. Under communist influence women left the seclusion of their homes and worked in the fields, took part as equals in political meetings and became active propagandists for the cause. Belden concluded that the emancipation of peasant women was economically important because it increased agricultural productivity, but it altered the power structure and psychology of the village much more profoundly (*China Shakes the World*, p. 420):

In many villages women exercised more power than men and very often they were much more passionate supporters of the Red Army than were their husbands and brothers.

The other group in society crucial to the success of the Chinese communist military and political success was the young. Most radical movements rely on the passion and idealism of youth, but in China their revolt was also directed against the domination of the young by the old in the hierarchy of society. Both Jack Belden and Edgar Snow formed the impression that quite a large number of Red Army soldiers joined up to escape marriages forced upon them by their elders, and others had rejected that filial piety which was the mainstay of this authoritarian system. One of Snow's portraits in *Red Star Over China* is of a man who suffered from the tyranny of his parents and his grandmother (Part 8, chapter 3, 'Why is a Red?'). The communist revolution was therefore in every sense a revolution of the young – Snow noted the extreme youth of the Red Army.

Once power has been won and the revolutionary government consolidated it is likely the momentum for change in social relations and attitudes will ebb and that, especially in areas less affected by the revolutionary struggle, traditional ideas will reassert themselves. C. K. Yang records numerous instances of the continued suppression and ill-treatment of women in China after 1949. One problem for a government committed to alter social relationships is how far it can use its authority to promote continuing progress towards egalitarianism without resorting to extensive coercion against those still holding to old attitudes. An even greater problem concerns sections of the population who supported the revolution, but gained what they wanted from it in the initial stages and have no wish to co-operate in further social changes designed to lead to communism: the obvious example here is the peasantry who acquire their own land after expropriating the landlords, who do not then wish to join the co-operatives or collectives. A third problem, which is related to the other two, is that the government can only alter social attitudes and beliefs – at least among future generations – by seeking to influence the values inculcated through education, through cultural activity and through the elaboration of political ideals. Yet in this area it runs the greatest danger of arbitrary censorship, propaganda and indoctrination, which conduce to the creation of an ideology which is used to bestow legitimacy on governmental abuse of power.

A government committed to revolutionary goals thus faces what appears to be an almost inescapable dilemma. On the one hand, as was argued in relation to the Yugoslav Party's attempt to move towards a partyless democracy, the realization of a wholly democratic and free society is dependent upon success in transforming social relations and attitudes. On the other it is precisely attempts to bring about this social transformation and to eliminate undesired legacies of the old order that pose the greatest challenge to extent and strength of the government's authority, so that governments committed to the furtherance of socialism have tended to fall back on use of terror or else to foster from above new class or generational conflicts, which contain their own dangers of arbitrary violence and ideological extremism, as was demonstrated in the Cultural Revolution in China.

It is possible to suggest that there is an inherent contradiction between the existence of a stable political authority and attempts to promote very rapid social change. Although the authority of a revolutionary party may derive in part from its claim to represent the values inherent in a future goal and although its authoritative role implies the right to initiate and influence the direction of social change, its ability to maintain authority and avoid resort to force depends upon retaining the support of the people. No revolutionary party has yet successfully resolved this problem of maintaining progress towards its ideal goals and maintaining genuine popular support and genuine authority while doing so.

Bibliography

ADCOCK, F. E., *Roman Political Ideas and Practice*, University of Michigan Press, Ann Arbor, 1963.

ARENDT, HANNAH, *The Human Condition*, Anchor Books, Doubleday, New York, 1959.

ARENDT, HANNAH, *Between Past and Future*, Faber & Faber, London, 1961.

ARISTOTLE, *The Politics* (ed. Ernest Barker), Oxford University Press, London, 1960.

BANTOCK, G. H., *Freedom and Authority in Education*, Faber & Faber, London, 1955.

BARROW, R. H., *The Romans*, Penguin, Harmondsworth, 1965.

BELDEN, JACK, *China Shakes the World*, Penguin, Harmondsworth, 1973.

BELL, DAVID R., 'Authority', in G. N. A. Vesey (ed.), *The Proper Study*, Royal Institute of Philosophy Lectures, vol. 3, 1971.

BURKE, EDMUND, *Reflections on the Revolution in France* (ed. Conor Cruise O'Brien), Penguin, Harmondsworth, 1968.

CARR, E. H., *The Bolshevik Revolution 1917–23*, vol. 1, Macmillan, London, 1950.

DAY, J., 'Authority', *Political Studies*, vol. II, no. 3, 1963.

DE JOUVENEL, BERTRAND, *The Pure Theory of Politics*, Cambridge University Press, 1963.

DE MAISTRE, J., *The Works of Joseph de Maistre* (ed. Jack Lively), Allen & Unwin, London, 1965.

DE TOCQUEVILLE, A., *Democracy in America* (ed. Richard Heffner), Mentor Books, New American Library, New York, 1956.

FAIRBANK, JOHN K., *The United States and China*, 3rd edn, Harvard University Press, Cambridge, Mass., 1971.

FAULKNER, WILLIAM, *Intruder in the Dust*, Chatto & Windus, London, 1957.

FITZGERALD, C. P., *Flood Tide in China*, Cresset Press, London, 1958.

FRIEDMAN, RICHARD B., 'On the Concept of Authority in Political Philosophy', in R. Flatham (ed.), *Concepts in Social and Political Philosophy*, Macmillan, New York, 1973.

FRIEDRICH, CARL J. (ed.), *Authority* (Nomos series, no. 1), Liberal Arts Press, Bobbs-Merrill, New York, 1958.

FRIEDRICH, CARL J., *Tradition and Authority*, Pall Mall, London, 1972.
FROMM, ERICH, *Fear of Freedom*, Routledge & Kegan Paul, London, 1960.
HARRIS, R. BAINES (ed.), *Authority: A Philosophical Analysis*, University of Alabama Press, 1976.
HOBBES, THOMAS, *Leviathan*, Collier Books edn, New York, 1962.
HOLT, JOHN, *Escape from Childhood*, Penguin, Harmondsworth, 1975.
HOMANS, GEORGE C., *The Human Group*, Routledge & Kegan Paul, London, 1951.
KANTOROWICZ, ERNST H., *The King's Two Bodies*, Princeton University Press, 1957.
KRIMERMAN, LEONARD I. and PERRY, LEWIS (eds), *Patterns of Anarchy*, Anchor Books, Doubleday, New York, 1966.
KROPOTKIN, PETER, *The State*, Freedom Press, London, 1946.
LAMPEDUSA, GIUSEPPE DI, *The Leopard*, Fontana Books, Collins, London, 1963.
LASKI, HAROLD J., *Authority in the Modern State*, Yale University Press, New Haven, 1919.
LOCKE, JOHN, *Two Treatises of Civil Government*, Dent, London, 1955.
LOEWENSTEIN, KARL, *Max Weber's Political Ideas in the Perspective of Our Time*, University of Massachusetts Press, Amherst, Mass., 1966.
MCILWAIN, CHARLES, *Constitutionalism: Ancient and Modern*, Cornell University Press, Ithaca, New York, 1947.
MAIR, LUCY, *Primitive Government*, Penguin, Harmondsworth, 1966.
MANN, THOMAS, *Stories of a Lifetime*, vol. 2, Secker & Warburg, London, 1961.
MARONGUI, ANTONIO, *Medieval Parliaments*, Eyre & Spottiswoode, London, 1968.
MILGRAM, STANLEY, *Obedience to Authority*, Tavistock, London, 1974.
NEILL, A. S., *Summerhill*, Gollancz, London, 1964.
NISBET, ROBERT A., *The Sociological Tradition*, Heinemann, London, 1971.
NISBET, ROBERT A., *The Twilight of Authority*, Heinemann, London, 1976.
PIPES, RICHARD (ed.), *Revolutionary Russia: A Symposium*, Anchor Books, Doubleday, New York, 1969.
PLATO, *The Republic of Plato* (ed. F. M. Cornford), Oxford University Press, London, 1969.
QUINTON, ANTHONY (ed.), *Political Philosophy*, Oxford University Press, London, 1967.
ROUSSEAU, JEAN-JACQUES, *The Social Contract*, Penguin, Harmondsworth, 1968.
SNOW, EDGAR, *Red Star Over China*, Penguin, Harmondsworth, 1972.
TROTSKY, LEON, *1905*, Penguin, Harmondsworth, 1973.
ULLMANN, WALTER, *A History of Political Thought in the Middle Ages*, Penguin, Harmondsworth, 1970.
VOEGELIN, E., *The New Science of Politics*, University of Chicago Press, 1952.
WEBER, MAX, *Theory of Economic and Social Organization* (ed. Talcott Parsons), Free Press, New York, 1964.
WELDON, T. D., *The Vocabulary of Politics*, Penguin, Harmondsworth, 1955.
WILLS, DAVID, *Spare the Child*, Penguin, Harmondsworth, 1971.
WRONG, DENNIS (ed.), *Max Weber*, Prentice-Hall, Englewood Cliffs, N.J., 1970.
YANG, C. K., *Chinese Communist Society: The Family and the Village*, MIT Press, Cambridge, Mass., 1965.

ECHEANCE   *DATE DUE*

UNIVERSITY OF SUDBURY
UNIVERSITE DE SUDBURY